On This Day

Elle Whyt

On This Day: Spurs by Elle Whyte
First Published 2020
© 2020 Elle Whyte

The author has made every effort to ensure the accuracy of this book at the time of publishing. Nevertheless, things change. If you notice any errors or changes that should be made to this book, please contact the publisher.

This is an unofficial Spurs book and is not associated with the football club.

ISBN: 9798662661622

For Chris, the biggest Spurs fan I know

January

1st January 2017: A day of firsts for Spurs hero Harry Kane who, in his 100th Premier League appearance, scored the first Premier League goal of the New Year in a game against Watford. Exactly two years later, on 1st January 2019, Kane scored the opening goal in an away game against Cardiff, becoming the first player to have scored against every Premier League team he had faced.

2nd January 2001: A frenzied Premiership clash against Newcastle United at White Hart Lane saw Spurs player Neil Sullivan and two Newcastle players sent off and three penalties awarded. Spurs emerged from the chaos with a 4-2 win, with goals from Gary Doherty, Sergei Rebrov, Les Ferdinand and Darren Anderton.

3rd January 2000: In an overcast and drizzly first game of the new millennium, Spurs beat Liverpool 1-0 at White Hart Lane. After missing a number of early chances, Chris Armstrong scored the winner when he picked the ball up 25 yards out before slamming a drive into the top corner in the 23rd minute.

4th January 2019: In the 3rd round of the FA Cup, Spurs beat League Two Tranmere Rovers 7-0, setting a record for the biggest away win in the club's history. Rovers unexpectedly kept us at bay for 40 minutes until Serge Aurier dramatically struck an unstoppable swerving goal into the top corner from 25 yards out. Then, in an explosive start to the second half, Fernando Llorente, Serge Aurier and the irrepressible Son Heung-Min hit home three goals within 9 minutes, before Llorente grabbed another two to complete his hat-trick. Harry Kane then scored the seventh, to become Spurs' joint fourth top scorer of all-time with 159 goals (joint with Cliff Jones).

5th January 2007: A wet and windy FA Cup 3rd round match against Championship team Cardiff ended in a goalless draw. Spurs relentlessly tried to prove their dominance, with Jermain Defoe and Dimitar Berbatov both being denied by the Cardiff keeper, but ultimately were unable to find the winner. Spurs went on to win the replay, to book their place in the 4th round against Southend.

6th January 1934: A brilliant display of attacking in a First Division match saw Spurs produce our biggest away win of the season, as we beat Aston Villa 5-1. Jimmy McCormick opened the scoring when he headed in from close range before three goals from Tom Meads, George Hunt and Les Howe put Spurs 4-0 up by half-time. In the second half, Spurs had to play with only 10 men after David Colqhoun was taken off with a head injury, but the team appeared unphased, as McCormick stepped up for a second time to score Spurs' fifth. Villa managed to scrape back a consolation goal in the final seconds to make the score 5-1, but their fans were less than impressed and pelted the players with fruit and bottles as they left the pitch.

7th January 1939: Spurs players wore numbered shirts for the first time in this 3rd round FA Cup match against Watford at White Hart Lane. Spurs won 7-1 thanks to goals from Ralph Ward (penalty), Fred Sargent, Willie Hall (2), Andy Duncan, and Les Miller (2). A few months after Spurs started playing in numbered shirts, the Football League Management Committee voted that all Football League games should be played in numbered shirts. However, the interruption of the Football League by the War meant that it wasn't actually until the 1946-47 season that all teams wore numbered shirts as standard practice.

8th January 1901: Our first game against an international European team was against the touring "German Association", although all the players were from Berlin FC. This was the first visit to Britain by a German football team. The friendly game ended in a 9-6 home win at a snow-covered White Hart Lane.

9th January 1905: In the semi-final of the Southern Charity Cup at White Hart Lane, we inflicted our best ever victory over West Ham. The match, which ended 10-0, saw goals from Sandy Tait (penalty), John Brearley (2) Vivian Woodward (5) and Charles O'Hagan (2). Vivian Woodward still holds the record for the most goals scored in a game between the two sides.

10th January 2016: An entertaining 3rd round FA Cup game ended with a 2-2 draw with Leicester. Christian Eriksen put Spurs ahead after just 8 minutes but Leicester levelled 11 minutes later. There was everything to play for in the second half which was played at an electric pace. Leicester quickly took the lead and appeared to be holding on, but Harry Kane secured us a replay with a late penalty, his 50th goal for Spurs.

11th January 1975: An emphatic 5-2 victory over Newcastle United at St James' Park was a welcome surprise for a struggling Spurs who, following the resignation of manager Bill Nicholson, continued to battle at the bottom of the table under new manager Terry Neill. Alfie Conn, the last player to be signed by Bill Nicholson, fired Spurs ahead after 14 minutes, before Cyril Knowles added a second with a cross that sent the United goalkeeper the wrong way. John Duncan and Alfie Conn then added another two in two minutes to put us 4-0 up by half-time. Duncan's goal was Tottenham's 4,000th goal in League football. Newcastle rallied after the break and managed to get a goal, but Conn got his hat-trick when Newcastle failed to clear Jimmy Neighbour's on-target back-header. Newcastle scored another, leaving the final score at 5-2.

12th January 1953: Following a 1-1 draw two days earlier, Spurs re-met Tranmere Rovers at WHL for this FA Cup 3rd round replay. Tranmere Rovers were a mid-table team in the Third Division North while Spurs were in the top half of the First Division. And Spurs made sure there was no mistaking their superiority, crushing Rovers 9-1. Once Baily had scored the first, the floodgates opened, with goals from McClellan (3), Duquemin (2), Hollis (2) and Baily (2). Les Medley worked hard to create many of the goals and was unfortunate not to score himself. Eddie Gibbins and Roy Hollis both made their debuts.

13th January 1900: Tom Pratt scored the first recorded penalty for the club in a Southern League match against Chatham at White Hart Lane that ended 2-1. Tom Smith scored our other goal. In the coming years, fans would be treated to some tremendous penalties. Jimmy Greaves was Spurs' top penalty scorer in the old First Division, whilst Harry Kane has led the scoreboard since the creation of the Premier League.

14th January 2007: In a controversial first-half disagreement, Pascal Chimbonda was shown a lenient yellow card for slapping Newcastle's Nicky Butt in the face with his glove. Spurs were relieved to get off lightly, but the incident appeared to galvanise the Newcastle players, who went on to win the game 3-2.

15th January 1914: Following a 5-5 draw against Leicester Fosse in the first round of the FA Cup, we won the replay 2-0 at White Hart Lane, with goals from Fanny Walden and Bert Bliss. Obviously impressed by his skills in this game, Spurs signed Leicester player Tommy Clay the following day.

16th January 1913: Following a 1-1 draw in an FA Cup home game against Blackpool, we went on to beat them 6-1 in the replay. This "away" replay was actually played at White Hart Lane, as Blackpool were struggling with poor ticket sales and so 'sold' their home game to Tottenham. The goals were scored by James Cantrell (2), Herbert Middlemiss, Robert Steel and Walter Tattersall (2).

17th January 1968: After becoming the most expensive player in England when he signed from Southampton for a record £125,000, Martin Chivers proved his worth when he scored on his Spurs debut at Hillsborough. Sheffield Wednesday took the lead but Jimmy Greaves equalised just before the break. The match remained 1-1 throughout most of the second half but, with minutes to go, Chivers powered through the Sheffield Wednesday defence to loop in the winner. Martin Chivers went on to score 174 goals in 367 matches for Spurs, and remains our fourth best goal-scorer of all time.

18th January 1947: Three days after sustaining a serious hip injury and concussion, Spurs goalkeeper Ted Ditchburn stood defiant as he fought off countless on-target shots in this League Division Two match at St James' Park. In the end, he only surrendered one goal to Newcastle and, at the final whistle, 63,000 Newcastle fans praised his valiant efforts with a standing ovation. A former boxer, Ditchburn was highly regarded for both his speed and strength and is remembered as one of Spurs' greatest ever goalkeepers. He made 452 appearances for Spurs, a club record that was held until 1975.

19th January 2006: Tottenham unveiled the new club badge, the first redesign since 1983. The badge also replaced the old club crest which had been introduced in 1956 to look more like the copper cockerel above the West Stand. The Cockerel and Ball symbol has become synonymous with Spurs and originated from "Harry Hotspur's" passion for cockfighting.

20th January 2016: After an initial draw, and with both sides flying high in the Premier League, this FA Cup 3rd round replay against

Leicester City promised to be a closely fought battle. Despite an uneventful opening, Son Heung-min broke the deadlock with a thunderous 18-yard strike in the 39th minute, before setting up another for Nacer Chadli. The impressive 2-0 away win saw us book a place in the FA Cup 4th round.

21st January 1967: A 2-0 home win against Burnley started a record run of 28 matches without defeat. The unbeaten games included 20 wins and 8 draws in 20 League and 8 FA Cup matches, including the FA Cup Final, and continued until 2nd September the following season with a thumping 1-5 defeat, incidentally, to Burnley.

22nd January 2008: In our first victory over Arsenal in nine years, we inflicted a spectacular 5-1 win in this League Cup semi-final match at White Hart Lane. Spurs got off to the perfect start when Jermaine Jenas angled in a low strike after just three minutes, and Woolwich FC generously doubled our lead with an own goal. With our rivals pushing for a way back into the game, Robbie Keane took advantage of their vulnerable defence to grab our third goal early in the second half. Aaron Lennon and Steed Malbranque then scored on either side of a consolation goal from Arsenal, to leave us 5-1 winners and book a place in the Final against defending champions Chelsea on 24th February.

23rd January 2002: Our first victory over Chelsea since 1989 was another 5-1 League Cup semi-final victory at White Hart Lane and was one of the greatest ever nights in Spurs history. Steffen Iversen scored the first goal to wipe out our deficit from the first leg. Spurs continued their defiant display, with four more goals from Tim Sherwood, Teddy Sheringham, Simon Davies and Sergei Rebrov, to book a place in the Cup Final.

24th January 1953: Sonny Walters scored our 1500th League goal at White Hart Lane as we beat Sheffield Wednesday 2-1. Eddie Baily scored the other goal. Sonny Walters initially signed for Spurs in 1944 and, after serving in the War, played for the club until 1957. Walters was part of Arthur Rowe's famous 'Push and Run' team that won the Second Division in 1950 and First Division in 1951 following promotion. During his time at Spurs, Walters made 234 appearances scoring 71 goals.

25th January 1964: Derek Possee, who replaced an injured Cliff Jones, marked his Spurs debut with a home goal in a 3-1 against Aston Villa. The other goals came from Terry Dyson and Jimmy Greaves. The win was Spurs' 800th league victory and maintained our position as First Division leaders, four points clear of second-place Blackburn Rovers.

26th January 1991: Spurs knocked Oxford United out of the FA Cup in this 4th round match at White Hart Lane. Paul Gascoigne was the star of the show and was involved in all four Tottenham goals, scoring two and setting up the other two for Gary Lineker and Gary Mabbutt. Following this 4-2 win, Spurs went on to win the 1991 FA Cup, our eighth victory in nine FA Cup Finals, and our first since 1982.

27th January 2018: In the FA Cup, Tottenham were drawn against League Two Newport County, and became the first top-flight team to play a competitive match at Newport since 1986. It was somewhat of a culture shock for Tottenham, swapping the plush Wembley stadium for the dilapidated ground that Newport County shared with two rugby teams. It should have been an easy win for Spurs, but the players appeared flustered by the impassioned Newport support and carelessly conceded a goal. Spurs stepped up their game in the second half and Harry Kane bagged an equaliser to save Spurs from FA Cup humiliation.

28th January 2017: A fantastically exciting 4th round FA Cup match against Wycombe started badly for Spurs when Wycombe went up 2-0 by half-time. Spurs pulled back level when Son scored on the hour and Vincent Janssen converted a penalty four minutes later. However, Wycombe restored their lead in the 84th minute and, with Spurs now down to 10 men, Wycombe already one foot in the 5th round. But in a show of absolute determination, Dele Alli pulled Spurs level with a composed goal in the 89th minute, before Son scrambled in a late winner deep into extra time to snatch a hugely deserved 4-3 victory.

29th January 1910: In Tottenham's first season in the top flight, the three Steel brothers played together for the first and only time in this match against Bradford City at White Hart Lane. Bobby Steel and Danny Steel were regular Spurs players during our first two seasons in the Football League and, for this game only, their brother, Alex, also made an appearance.

30th January 1904: A 7-4 win over Reading became our highest aggregate score in a Southern League game. Before joining the Football League in 1908, Spurs played in three regional Leagues, the Southern League, the Western League, and the London League.

31st January 2018: In a League match against Manchester United at Wembley Stadium, Christian Erikson scored within 11 seconds of kick-off to become the third-fastest goal-scorer in Premier League history, after Alan Shearer and former Spurs captain Ledley King. Eriksen's aggressive opening goal caught the United players off guard, and Spurs took advantage of their stunned opposition to grab a deserved 2-0 victory. This was Tottenham's third successive home League game against Manchester United, a feat not achieved since 1966.

February

1st February 1899: Following an initial 1-1 draw at White Hart Lane, we beat Newton Heath 5-3 and knocked them out of the FA Cup in the first round. Newton Heath was later renamed Manchester United, making this our first-ever win over the Red Devils.

2nd February 2019: In this game of deadlock, Spurs eventually managed to break down the heavy Newcastle defence, when Son Heung-min scored a powerful 20-yard winner seven minutes from time. This match was Vertonghen's 200th Premier League game for Spurs, the 12th player to reach this milestone. The win was Spurs' 29th consecutive game without a draw, setting a new Premier League record. Spurs would go on to extend this streak to 32 games between 9th May 2018 and 27 February 2019.

3rd February 1960: Spurs recorded their biggest ever win in this FA Cup 4th round replay when they beat Fourth Division Crewe Alexandra 13-2 at White Hart Lane. Bobby Smith opened the scoring in the 3rd minute, then Les Allen got the second. Smith scored again two minutes later before Crewe pulled a goal back to make it 3-1. A further seven goals from Tommy Harmer, Les Allen (3), Bobby Smith (2) and Cliff Jones brought the score up to 10-1 by half time. After the break, Jones grabbed his second, and Allen scored his fifth. Crewe salvaged one back, but a penalty from Jones ten minutes from time completed his hat-trick to see Spurs win 13-2. Legend has it that Crewe arrived at London Euston station that day on platform 13 and left again from number 2.

4th February 2018: Harry Kane scored his 100th Premier League goal when he converted an added-time penalty to secure a 2-2 draw with Liverpool at Anfield. Kane achieved this milestone in just 141 games, a record only beaten by Alan Shearer, who achieved the feat in 124 goals more than 20 years earlier.

5th February 1927: Two weeks after the first-ever live radio broadcast of a football match between Arsenal and Sheffield United, BBC radio broadcast a Tottenham match for the first time. It was a First Division match against Sunderland at White Hart Lane that we lost 2-0.

6th February 1982: To celebrate the official opening of the new West Stand, we made a triumphant 6-1 victory over Wolverhampton Wanderers. Ricky Villa scored a hat-trick. The new West Stand was formally opened by Sir Stanley Rous, the former FIFA president.

7th February 1993: In a Premiership game at White Hart Lane, Spurs came from behind to beat Southampton 4-2. After a disappointing first half, in which the visitors took an early lead, Tottenham emerged from the interval with newfound vigour, scoring four goals in a five minute period. Sheringham scored two, and Nick Barmby and Darren Anderton got the other two. Despite the four-goal blitz being down to 10 players, Southampton valiantly fought back to score a second.

8th February 1899: Spurs' first manager, Frank Brettell, announced he was moving to the newly-formed Portsmouth, who had offered him substantially more money. He had only taken up the post less than a year earlier. John Cameron, who Brettell had signed from Everton, took over as manager after Bretell left.

9th February 1929: Spurs beat Port Vale 4-2 in a League Division Two match, with goals from Frederick Barnett, Jimmy Dimmock and Frank Osborne (2). The match was Arthur Grimsdell's final appearance for

Spurs before moving to Clapton Orient. Grimsdell is still regarded as one of Spurs' best-ever players, and was propelled to celebrity status when he captained the team that won the Second Division title in 1920 and the FA Cup in 1921. In total, Grimsell made 418 appearances for Tottenham, scoring 43 goals.

10th February 2018: A Premier League record crowd of 83,222 fans packed into Wembley Stadium to watch Spurs beat Arsenal 1-0 in the 195th North London Derby. The crowd was just short of the Football League record of 83,260 set by Manchester United in the old First Division in 1948, also against Arsenal. Arsenal kept Spurs at bay in the first half with their strong defence, but we broke through after the break with Kane's superb towering header in the 49th minute. This was Kane's 101st Premier League goal and his seventh goal in seven league games against Arsenal.

11th February 2012: Striker Emmanuel Adebayor made a record four Premier League assists in this 5-0 win against Newcastle United at White Hart Lane. Benoit Assou-Ekotto opened the scoring at just 4 minutes, after being picked out unmarked by Adebayor. Two minutes later, Adebayor crossed for debutant Louis Saha to volley home, before assisting Saha again on 20 minutes. Adebayor's own shot on target was saved, and Niko Kranjcar side-footed in the rebound to put us 4-0 up by half-time. On 64 minutes, Adebayor volleyed home to finally grab the goal his performance deserved. The elated home crowd piled on the support for manager Harry Redknapp, who had also just been cleared of tax evasion charges. At the time, Redknapp was the top favourite to become the next England manager, and the Spurs fans called out for their hero to stay. At the final whistle, an emotional Redknapp waved his gratitude to all four corners of the ground.

12th February 1944: Jack Rowley, a guest player from Manchester United, netted a club-record seven goals, as we beat Luton Town 8-1.

During the War, League football was suspended and replaced with two regional Wartime Leagues, with clubs bringing in guest players to provide much-needed entertainment.

13th February 1901: Southern League Spurs met First Division Preston in the first round of the FA Cup. Following a 1-1 draw in the first leg at White Hart Lane, Spurs appeared the stronger side in this replay. Player-manager John Cameron opened the scoring after just six minutes, and another two goals from Sandy Brown gave Spurs a 3-0 lead by half-time. In the second half, Preston scored twice, but Brown completed his hat-trick, to end the game with a 4-2 win. The eleven players who won at Preston went on to play in all of the remaining FA Cup matches on the way to FA Cup glory. On winning the title, Spurs became the first and only club from outside the Football League to ever win the FA Cup.

14th February 2013: Gareth Bale scored a free-kick in the last minute of each half to see us beat Olympique Lyonnais 2-1 in a Europa League match at White Hart Lane. After missing an open goal early in the game, Bale brought White Hart Lane to its feet with a swerving 35-yard strike in first-half injury time. Lyon equalised early in the second half but, in the dying seconds of the game, curled in another free-kick for the win.

15th February 2011: one of the greatest results in our history was a 1-0 away win over the prestigious AC Milan in the 1st leg of the UEFA Champions League last 16. Peter Crouch knocked in the winner after 80 minutes, but Spurs keeper Heurelho Gomes was the hero making two superb saves. Although the Spanish legends played well below their usual standard, Spurs fans still felt immense pride in overcoming a club of such renown.

16th February 2020: In a bizarre opening, Spurs defender Toby Alderweireld scored an own goal in the 9th minute of this game against Aston Villa. As penance for his error, Alderweireld quickly turned it around to score for Spurs. Another two goals from Son earnt Spurs a 3–2 victory at Villa Park. With these goals, Son became the first Asian footballer to score 50 goals in the Premier League, with 51 scored goals in 151 Premier League matches.

17th February 1899: John Cameron became manager whilst still playing for the club, taking over from Frank Brettel who had signed Cameron the year before. In his first game in charge, Cameron's winning goal saw Tottenham become the first lower-tier club to come from behind to win an FA cup tie against a League One team. In the following seasons, Cameron led Tottenham to the 1900 Southern League title and then to the 1901 FA Cup title, becoming the only non-Football League team to lift the trophy.

18th February 1958: Tottenham signed Welsh international Cliff Jones from Swansea. Jones would go on to score 159 goals in 378 appearances during his ten years with Spurs and remains our fifth-best goal-scorer of all time. Jones was also a crucial member of the 1961 "Double"-winning side.

19th February 2017: In the fifth round of the FA Cup, Harry Kane scored all three goals as we beat Fulham 3-0. The frantic opening was a demonstration of how much both teams wanted a place in the quarter-finals, but Harry Kane, Christian Eriksen and Kieran Trippier combined to form an effective attacking trio, setting up two goals for Kane. Kane then came back for his third, grabbing his second hat-trick of 2017 and his fifth for Spurs.

20th February 2015: A long-running dispute finally came to an end when Archway Sheet Metal Works, a local business standing in the way of Tottenham Hotspur's new £400m stadium, lost its High Court battle against a compulsory purchase order. The battle against the family-run firm had been bitter and, the previous year, a mysterious fire had gutted the company's offices, with the owners suspecting arson. The court case was heard by The Hon. Mr. Justice Dove, a self-proclaimed Aston Villa fan.

21st February 1976: In a First Division match against Stoke City, Glenn Hoddle made his Spurs debut. Stoke took the lead but John Duncan equalised. Then in a perfect start to his exceptional Spurs career, Hoddle ensured his arrival did not go unnoticed when he scored a spectacular long-range strike for the win.

22nd February 1937: In an incredible come-back, Spurs beat Everton 4-3 in a dramatic FA Cup replay. Everton took control with a two-goal lead. Johnny Morrison pulled one back for Spurs but Everton scored again after the break. As the match drew to a close, Everton remained 3-1 up and Spurs looked to be heading out of the Cup. But in a dramatic comeback, Morrison scored his second before Joe Meek grabbed the equaliser with just two minutes remaining. Then in the final glorious minute, Morrison completed his second hat-trick of the tournament for an incredible Spurs come-back.

23rd February 2009: A 2–1 win against Hull City at the KC Stadium helped to ease Tottenham's relegation fears. In an entertaining first half, Spurs took an early lead after Aaron Lennon's superb 20-yard strike, but the Tigers clawed back an equaliser 10 minutes later after Spurs keeper Carlo Cudicini fumbled a corner. The game then went into a stalemate, but with four minutes to go, Jonathan Woodgate, in his 50th Spurs appearance, strode forward to head in Benoit Assou-Ekotto's cross for the winner.

24th February 2008: This was the first League Cup Final to be played at the new Wembley Stadium, and the first to be played in England since the old Wembley was demolished in 2000. We faced Chelsea, who opened the scoring early, but Dimitar Berbatov brought us back level. Jonathan Woodgate struck in the winner in extra time, to hand Spurs our fourth League Cup title, and first since 1999. Juande Ramos also continued his record of never being beaten in a Cup Final, having previously won five times with Sevilla.

25th February 2013: Gareth Bale produced a stunning world-class performance as we beat West Ham 3-2. Bale opened the scoring with a powerful strike before the Hammers scored two to take the lead. Gylfi Sigurdsson brought Spurs back level, then, in the dying seconds, Bale sealed the victory with a stunning 30-yard strike into the top corner of the net. This was Bale's 11th away goal of the season, more than any Premiership player.

26th February 2017: In a 4-0 victory over Stoke, Harry Kane scored three of the goals. This was Kane's third hat-trick in nine games, and his second in consecutive domestic games. The first of these goals was his 100th in club football.

27th February 1971: In Spurs' first League Cup Final, we faced Third Division Aston Villa at Wembley. Villa proved a harder nut to crack than their Third Division status would suggest, but Bill Nicholson's team eventually found a way to break the deadlock with two late goals from Martin Chivers, to see us lift the Cup.

28th February 1927: Billy Minter took over as manager when Peter McWilliam left for Middlesbrough. In Minter's first season in charge, Spurs was relegated to the Second Division, which was unlucky as we finished only six points behind fourth-place Derby, and our 38 points was a record number of points for a relegated club at a time when it was only two points gained for a win. One crucial factor contributing to the relegation may have been Minter's decision to sell Jimmy Seed, believing that he was approaching the end of his career. Seed was transferred to Sheffield Wednesday who were struggling at the bottom of the table but, following his arrival, Wednesday beat Tottenham twice and avoided relegation, whilst Spurs were sent down.

March

1st March 2009: The League Cup Final at Wembley Stadium between Tottenham and Manchester United looked set to be a fiercely competitive match. Spurs were the reigning champions and each team had one of the two joint-top goalscorers of the tournament, with Spurs' Roman Pavlyuchenko having scored in every match so far. Despite the hype, the match ended in a disappointing goalless draw, taking the match to a penalty shoot-out for only the second time in history. Predictably, Spurs did not perform well, and Manchester United won the Cup 4–1 on penalties.

2nd March 1898: The Tottenham Hotspur Football and Athletic Company was registered as a Limited company. 8000 shares were issued at a price of £1 each, but only 1,558 were sold in the first year.

3rd March 1973: Tottenham won the League Cup Final for the second time in three years, beating Norwich City 1–0 at Wembley. Substitute Ralph Coates, who came off the bench following a John Pratt injury, scored the winning goal at 72 minutes, with a low shot into the left corner of the net. And in a show of dominance, exactly a week later, Spurs would beat Norwich City again in a League match at the Lane.

4th March 1949: Harry Clarke was signed as a defender. Clarke spent his entire senior career at Spurs, playing a total of 322 matches and netting four goals. He was a key member of Arthur Rowe's 'push-and-run' side of the early 1950s and played in all 42 matches of the 1950-51 season in which we won the League Title.

5th March 1938: Record attendance at White Hart Lane as 75,038 watched an FA Cup 6th round replay against Sunderland. The stadium was so packed that, even before the game, the police had to ease the crush in the stands. Kickoff was delayed while the touchline was cleared of spectators, and then during the game, the police had to clear space for the kicker each time a corner was taken. Despite the riotous home support, Sunderland scored ten minutes from time to win 1-0. Of the seven FA Cup matches against Spurs, this is the only one that Sunderland has ever won.

6th March 1985: An unfortunate 1-0 defeat to Real Madrid in a UEFA Cup 4th round tie is one of only a couple of occasions that we have lost a European match on home turf. Real Madrid was not the team it is today and was struggling with huge debts. But in an unexpected blow for new manager Peter Shreeves, Steve Perryman fluffed a save just 14 minutes in and looked horrified as the ball bounced into his net. Spurs were unable to find a way back into the game, letting Real slip through the net and paving their way to the UEFA Cup title. Shreeves should have taken Tottenham back to Europe the following year, but in an unfortunate turn of events, all English clubs were banned from the competition following the Heysel Stadium disaster.

7th March 1908: Billy Minter made his Spurs debut in a match against Millwall. In Spurs' first season in the Football League, Minter scored 16 goals, helping the club to gain promotion to the First Division. In his 12 years at Spurs, Minter made 334 appearances and was the club's top goalscorer until his record of 101 goals was broken by Jimmy Dimmock in 1930. Minter would later take over as manager.

8th March 1961: In an FA Cup 6th round replay, we defeated Sunderland 5-0, with goals from Bobby Smith, Les Allen, Terry Dyson (2) and Dave Mackay. A crowd of 64,797 supporters packed into White Hart Lane, many of whom had queued for ten hours to get in.

The 1-1 draw in the first game 4 days earlier had been a wake-up call for Spurs, who were desperate to reach the Final, having not been in an FA Cup final since their win in 1921. In an emphatic display of intent, Spurs went three goals ahead by half-time thanks to Les Allen, Bobby Smith and Terry Dyson. After the interval, Dyson scored his second with a header on 65 minutes and, five minutes later, Dave Mackay completed the scoring, as Spurs swept majestically into the semi-final against Burnley.

9th March 1946: In this Wartime League match at Fulham, we drew 1-1, with Spurs player Charlie Whitchurch scoring the first goal of the match. Len Duquemin made his debut in this match, the start of his brilliant decade-long career at Tottenham, in which he would make 307 appearances and score 134 goals. Duquemin was a cornerstone of Arthur Rowe's successful "push and run" side of the early 1950s. Known as 'Reliable Len', for his hard work rather than stylish play, his value was seen in his ability to create space for some of his more renowned teammates.

10th March 1919: A meeting between Football League chairmen decided that Spurs should be unfairly relegated in favour of Second Division Arsenal. Following the suspension of the Football League during the War, it had been decided that the First Division should be expanded by two teams, from 20 to 22 clubs. During previous expansions, this had been done simply by promoting the top Second Division sides without relegating any teams from the top flight. However, on this occasion, whilst 19th place Chelsea were allowed to stay, bottom-place Spurs were relegated. It was an unprecedented move led by Liverpool Chairman, John McKenna, who somehow persuaded the meeting attendees that Arsenal, who had finished 5th in Division Two, should be promoted as recognition for their long service to the League. It has later been implied that the Arsenal chairman Sir Henry Norris had bribed other club chairmen. And so whilst Arsenal now claims to hold the record for the longest time spent in the top flight, ironically the scum never actually earned their place. For the record, that season we immediately finished top of Division Two and were promptly promoted back to our rightful place.

11th March 2000: Spurs thrashed a struggling Southampton 7-2 in a Premier League game at White Hart Lane. The visitors got off to a decisive start, scoring three goals. Unfortunately for them, one of these goals was an own goal and once on the scoreboard, the floodgates opened for Spurs. Three goals in a spectacular six-minute period from Darren Anderton, Chris Armstrong and Steffan Iverson put us 4-2 up by half time. After the interval, Spurs' performance was little more than a primal display of their superiority. Chris Armstrong grabbed his second and Steffan Iversen completed a hat-trick to bring the final score to 7-2.

12th March 2017: In this FA Cup quarter-final against Millwall, Spurs produced an easy 6-0 win that saw us breeze into the semi-finals. Harry Kane went off with an ankle injury after just seven minutes, but the disappointment did not last long as his substitute, Christian Eriksen, came off the bench and quickly opened the scoring. Son scored either side of half-time and Dele tapped home the fourth. Substitute Vincent Janssen added the fifth before Son completed his first Spurs hat-trick in the dying seconds of the game.

13th March 1936: An article in the Weekly Herald reported, "Spurs are giving a month's trial to an amateur Wm. E. Nicholson, an inside right of Scarborough Working Man's Club. He recently celebrated his 17th birthday. His height is 5ft 8 ins and weight 10st 12 lbs." Bill Nicholson is now considered one of the greatest-ever figures in Spurs history, winning more football competitions than any other Spurs manager, and famously guiding the club to the "Double" win in 1961.

14th March 1929: Ted Harper signed from Sheffield Wednesday. In his 63 League appearances between 1929 and 1931, Harper scored an average of one goal per game and set a club record when he scored 36 goals in the 1930-31 season.

15th March 1987: A difficult FA Cup 6th round match at Wimbledon finished in a 2-0 victory thanks to goals from the famous duo Hoddle and Waddle. The game looked set to go to a goalless draw, but a late 84th-minute goal from Glenn Hoddle, and Chris Waddle's stunning long-range free-kick four minutes later, took Spurs into the semi-finals. The match was dedicated to full-back Danny Thomas who had suffered a serious knee injury the previous weekend. Thomas never recovered from the injury and was forced to retire the following year.

16th March 1985: Not since 1912, a month before the sinking of the Titanic, had Tottenham won at Anfield. For 73 long years, we had to endure endless jibes comparing our tragic away record against Liverpool with the Titanic disaster. But exactly 73 years to the day after our last win at Anfield, Peter Shreeve's team finally brought the taunts to an end with a long-awaited victory, thanks to Garth Crooks' winning goal, that was celebrated wildly by Spurs fans. Tottenham finished the season in third place, level on points with second-placed Liverpool. This would normally have earned us a place in the UEFA Cup but, in an unfortunate turn of events, that year all English clubs were banned from the competition following the Heysel Stadium disaster.

17th March 2007: Goalkeeper Paul Robinson scored the second goal of his career in a Premier League match against Watford at White Hart Lane. He took a free-kick from 95 yards and the ball bounced over the Watford goalkeeper straight into the goal. He became the third of only five Premier League goalkeepers to score in history.

18th March 1961: In the FA Cup semi-final, Spurs battled against reigning champions Burnley to earn a place in the Final. Spurs took the lead with a goal from Bobby Smith after 30 minutes, then doubled their lead with another from Smith after the break. Cliff Jones added the third before the end, as Spurs ran out with a 3-0 win at Villa Park. We were on the way to our first FA Cup Final at Wembley.

19th March 2005: In a lucky win, we beat Manchester City 2-1 at the Lane. Spurs took the lead when Jermain Defoe nodded in Simon Davies' miss, but City levelled with a brilliant volley. Keane then struck home in the 84th minute for the win.

20th March 2008: An exciting eight-goal match at White Hart Lane, ended in a 4-4 draw with Chelsea in the Premier League. Chelsea scored first but Spurs' Jonathon Woodgate quickly equalised when he headed in a free-kick. With defence low on the agenda, the game continued at an electrifying pace. Chelsea restored their lead before the break and, seven minutes into the second half, they seemed to have it in the bag as they made it 3-1. But, since the departure of Jose Mourinho, Chelsea was developing a habit of letting leads slip. A Berbatov header made it 3-2 before Tom Huddlestone brought us back level after a scramble with 15 minutes remaining. But the game was far from over. Chelsea quickly pulled back their lead and, with just two minutes remaining, Robbie Keane curled in a stunning long-range shot that left the final score at 4-4.

21st March 1999: A 1-0 victory in the League Cup Final at Wembley earnt us our first trophy in eight years. Justin Edinburgh was shown an unfortunate red card after Robbie Savage theatrically clutched his face after Edinburgh accidentally caught his hair. The undeserved red card meant we faced at least 30 minutes more play with only 10 men. But, like heroes, we held them off and with seconds to spare, deep into injury time, Allan Nielsen headed home to clinch glory and secure our third Football League Cup triumph.

22nd March 2008: Spurs were playing well this season, scoring an average of over 3 goals per game and, as the heavens opened in a torrential hail storm, the White Hart Lane faithful anticipated another flood of goals against Portsmouth. But despite Spurs' tidy possession that saw them dominate the first half, they could not manage to edge ahead. On 70 minutes, manager Juande Ramos brought Bent and Jamie O'Hara off the bench, and 10 minutes later Bent headed home Berbatov's scuffed shot, scoring the 100th Spurs goal of the Premier League season. Then just two minutes later, Bent set up another for Jamie O'Hara, who tapped gleefully home, to give us a deserved 2-0 win over Portsmouth.

23rd March 2014: In this game of two halves, Southampton dominated the first half, taking a confident two-goal lead. After the break, Spurs made a spirited comeback, with two close-range goals from Christian Eriksen pulling us back into the game. The game looked set to end on a draw until substitute Gylfi Sigurdsson struck in a dramatic long-distance winner in injury time to earn a thrilling 3-2 victory.

24th March 1979: In a 3-2 victory at Aston Villa, Tottenham scored their 1,000th away point in the Football League. In the same dramatic style as "yesterday's" match, Spurs came back from 2-0 down with just 12 minutes remaining, to win 3-2 with late goals from Glenn Hoddle (2) and Chris Jones.

25th March 1978: Under an almighty downpour, we faced Mansfield, who were struggling at the bottom of the Second Division. But Mansfield were desperately fighting to escape relegation and weren't going to let us take them down easily. In a fiercely battled match,

Mansfield raised their game and secured a 3-3 draw against the mighty Spurs. In an echo of "yesterday's" goalscorers, Glenn Hoddle scored two and Chris Jones scored another

26th March 1921: Tottenham had three games scheduled over the Easter weekend. During the 1-1 Good Friday match against Liverpool at Anfield, keeper Alex Hunter had been injured, meaning that he couldn't play against Sunderland the following day. And in the days before substitutes, Tommy Clay, normally a full-back, had to play the whole match in goal. Amazingly, the game ended in a 1-0 win, with Jimmy Seed scoring for Spurs.

27th March 1965: In an 11-goal thriller at White Hart LaneTottenham scored seven goals against Wolverhampton Wanderers, continuing their unbeaten home record. Our seven goals were scored by Eddie Clayton, Les Allen, Alan Gilzean (2) and Cliff Jones (3). Surprisingly, although playing, the usually prolific Jimmy Greaves did not score.

28th March 1998: Spurs arrived at Selhurst Park sitting in 17th place, five points ahead of opposition Crystal Palace, who languished in bottom place. Palace threw everything they had into the game but, while desperately trying to run us ragged, they were running themselves into the ground. Their players, out of position and out of breath, were unable to sustain their strong defensive wall, allowing Spurs into the game. Ten minutes into the second-half, Nicola Berti broke through, his looping header deceiving the Palace keeper. Then former Palace striker Chris Armstrong came back to haunt the Palace fans when he produced a spectacular diving header that killed off any dreams of surviving relegation. Jurgen Klinsmann scored a third in the 77th minute. Palace pulled back a late consolation but it was too little too late, as Spurs won 3-1.

29th March 1958: Bobby Smith scored four and Terry Medwin scored two, as we beat Aston Villa 6-2. Bobby Smith netted our 1,000th home goal in the First Division. The prolific Bobby Smith scored 208 goals in 317 appearances for the club and remains our second highest goal-scorer of all time, behind Jimmy Greaves.

30th March 2013: Spurs leapfrogged over Chelsea up to 3rd place in the Premier league table following an impressive 2-1 win over Swansea at the Liberty Stadium. We had an excellent start, scoring two goals in the first 21 minutes, thanks to Jan Vertonghen and Gareth Bale. The 2-1 victory, Spurs' 9th away win of the Premier League season, extended the club record.

31st March 2019: In this Premier League game against Liverpool at Anfield, Liverpool took an early lead. The game continued on a tense knife-edge until Lucas Moura pulled back an equaliser in the 70th minute. Christian Eriksen's assist in Moura's goal saw him become only the second player ever, after David Beckham, to record more than 10 assists in four consecutive Premier League seasons. As the match drew to a close, the game seemed to be heading to a draw, but in an agonising last-minute blunder, Spurs defender Toby Alderweireld accidentally nudged in an own goal after Hugo Lloris fielded a header into his path. The mistake not only handed Liverpool the win but also sent them back to the top of the table.

April

1st April 2018: A 3-1 victory over Chelsea was our first
at Stamford Bridge. Chelsea took the lead, but Ch
equalised with a stunning 30-yard strike just before the i al. It was
a different game after the break and Dele Alli, in his 100th Premier
League appearance, struck twice in four minutes. Manager Mauricio
Pochettino praised Dele as a "fighter" after suffering a disappointing
couple of weeks with the England team.

2nd April 2005: In this Premier League away game, Birmingham
player Jermaine Pennant came on wearing an electronic ankle-tag after
being released from prison for drink-driving, driving while
disqualified, and driving without insurance. Pennant played well on his
comeback and was given a standing ovation by the home crowd when
he was substituted after 55 minutes. However, 'The Campaign
Against Drink Driving' was less impressed and voiced their serious
disapproval that Pennant had been allowed to play. Stephen Kelly
netted Spurs a goal on 59 minutes but the hosts quickly levelled in this
1-1 draw.

3rd April 2019: Official opening of the magnificent new £1 billion
Tottenham Hotspur stadium. With a giant golden cockerel
illuminating in the night sky above the opening ceremony, the
atmosphere was electric. A local school choir performed "Everybody
Dreams", which was written as an anthem of hope for the area after the
London riots in 2011. After the ceremony, Spurs kicked off their first
home match on the site for 689 days, playing against Crystal Palace.
And on 55 minutes, Son Heung-min scored the first goal at the new
stadium. Christian Eriksen, in his 200th Premier League appearance,

...red the second when he scrambled home from close range, to ...nd off the perfect night with a 2-0 victory.

4th April 1914: Spurs winger Fanny Walden made his England international debut in a match against Scotland and, at only 5' 2" tall, became the shortest England player. Walden was a key member of the Spurs team that won the Second Division title in 1920, but an unfortunately-timed injury meant he missed the 1921 FA Cup Final. Walden made more than 300 appearances for Spurs, including in 214 League games and 22 FA Cup matches.

5th April 2017: In a sensational last-minute turnaround, Spurs came from 1-0 down at 88 minutes to beat Swansea 3-1. Dele Alli drew Spurs level, before Son Heung-min put us ahead three minutes later. Christian Eriksen then struck in the third to seal the victory.

6th April 1901: Vivian Woodward made his Southern League debut for Spurs. In his nine seasons at the club, Woodward made 169 appearances and scored 73 goals. After the club was elected to the Football League in 1908, Woodward scored our first-ever League goal in a match against Wolverhampton Wanderers. He was the first Spur to gain a Full England cap and captained England as well as the Great British Olympic team in 1908 and 1912. During the War, Woodward sustained an injury to his right thigh and was unable to return to top-level football.

7th April 2014: In Harry Kane's first Premier League start for Tottenham, an eventful game saw us beat Sunderland 5-1 at the Lane. Sunderland opened the scoring, but Emmanuel Adebayor equalised from Christian Eriksen's cross. Eriksen then assisted Kane, who guided the ball home for his first-ever Premier League goal. Eriksen then grabbed the goal his play deserved, before Adebayor got his second. Gylfi Sigurdsson wrapped up the scoring for a triumphant 5-1 victory.

8th April 1898: A record crowd of 15,000 spectators gathered at Northumberland Park to watch us play Woolwich Arsenal. Northumberland Park had been our home ground since moving from Tottenham Marshes in 1888. We shared the pitch with the UCH rugby team. Much of the land in this area was owned by the Percy family, descendants of the 1st Earl of Northumberland and his eldest son "Harry Hotspur". With the increasing crowds, a year after this match, the club moved to a piece of land to the east of Tottenham High Road, behind the White Hart pub.

9th April 1921: In an international match between England and Scotland, the England team featured four Spurs players: Bert Bliss, Jimmy Dimmock, Arthur Grimsdell and Bert Smith. Over the years, Tottenham have provided an incredible 78 England International players, more than any club.

10th April 2016: Our spectacular 3–0 home win over Manchester United was our first home League win against United since 2001. Kick-off was delayed as the United bus got stuck in the London traffic, but after waiting 15 years for this moment, Spurs were unphased by another 30 minutes. The game took a little time to get going, but in the second half, goals from Dele Alli, Toby Alderweireld and Erik Lamela saw Tottenham score three times in just 6 minutes. United barely threatened, taking until the 62nd minute to test goalkeeper Lloris.

11th April 1959: Dave Mackay gained the first Scottish cap by a Spurs player, in a match against England. Mackay made 268 league appearances for Spurs, winning one League Championship, three FA Cups, one European Cup Winners' Cup and two FA Charity Shields. Manager Bill Nicholson has since named Mackay as his best-ever signing.

12th April 2014: In a thrilling away game against West Brom, Spurs staged a storming come-back, pulling back from 3-0 down, with a West Brom own goal, Harry Kane's header, and Eriksen's stoppage-time equaliser, to draw 3-3.

13th April 2019: Lucas Moura scored the first hat-trick at the new stadium, as Mauricio Pochettino's side thrashed already-relegated Huddersfield 4-0. With Harry Kane injured and Son Heung-min rested ahead of the upcoming Champions League clash with Manchester City, Mauricio Pochettino made seven changes to the usual team. Despite the changes, Spurs dominated and piled on the pressure. Victor Wanyama slotted home midway through the first half to take Spurs into a deserved lead, before Moura added a second with a devilishly low shot less than 3 minutes later. In the 87th minute, Moura volleyed in his second, assisted by Christian Eriksen, who registered his 60th Premier League assist, eight more than any other player. Moura then completed his hat-trick in injury-time, the first hat-trick to be scored at the new Tottenham Hotspur Stadium.

14th April 1991: In this unforgettable game, we beat Arsenal 3-1 in the first FA Cup semi-final at Wembley. Spurs took an early lead with goals from Paul Gascoigne and Gary Lineker. This was Gazza at his peak, and his sublime 30-yard unstoppable drive in this game is possibly one of Spurs's greatest ever moments. Arsenal pulled one back, but Gary Lineker bagged another for a 3-1 win to take us to the Final.

15th April 2017: A 4-0 victory over Bournemouth gave Spurs seven consecutive Premier League wins, our longest run since 1967. In the first half, Mousa Dembele fired Spurs ahead from close range, before Son Heung-min's darting run and neat finish doubled the lead less than 3 minutes later. Harry Kane struck home early into the second half, before substitute Vincent Janssen capped off the win with a bonus injury-time goal. Kane's goal made him only the fourth player to score 20 Premier League goals in three consecutive seasons, after Alan Shearer, Ruud van Nistelrooy and Thierry Henry.

16th April 2005: This match at Anfield started with an impeccably observed minute's silence in remembrance of the 96 Liverpool fans who died in the Hillsborough tragedy on 15 April 1989. At kick-off, Spurs were the better team, dominating a lethargic-looking home side, and Erik Edman scored a spectacular 35-yard strike into the top-right corner that left the Liverpool keeper helpless. As the first half wore on, the Reds slowly woke from their stupor, pulling one back to level. A deflected Robbie Keane header put Spurs back in the lead, but Liverpool scored another for a 2-2 draw. Michael Dawson made his Spurs debut

17th April 1961: Reigning champions Tottenham won the League Cup for a second year in a row when we beat Sheffield Wednesday 2-1 in the Cup Final at White Hart Lane. Wednesday took the lead, but just before the break, Bobby Smith brought Spurs level and Les Allen grabbed a second a minute later. The victory secured the first half of the 1961 'Double' win, as we would later also become FA Cup champions.

18th April 1987: Glenn Hoddle and Chris Waddle's hit single "Diamond Lights" made its debut in the UK singles chart. The record spent eight weeks in the charts and peaked at number 12. Despite its success in the charts, the song was widely ridiculed, particularly after the mulletted duo's live performance on Top of the Pops. A Metro article titled "Top 10 worst sport songs ever" described the record as "truly awful dad dancing and shocking lyrics".

19th April 2015: Harry Kane scored his 30th goal of the season in a 3-1 win against Newcastle United at St James' Park, making him the first Tottenham player to reach the milestone since Gary Lineker in 1992.

20th April 1901: Southern League Tottenham Hotspur played in their first FA Cup Final, against Sheffield United at Crystal Palace. It was also the first FA Cup Final to be filmed by Pathé News. The official attendance was a world-record 110,820 although thousands more gained entrance. Sheffield United opened the scoring, but Sandy Brown quickly headed in an equaliser, leaving the score 1-1 at half time. Brown put Spurs ahead early in the second half, but Sheffield headed an equaliser for a 2-2 draw, taking the game to a replay the following week. Tottenham won the replay 3-1, becoming the first and, to date, only club outside the top two divisions to win the FA Cup.

21st April 1923: Jimmy Cantrell made his last League appearance for Spurs in this match against Birmingham City. At 40 years and 349 days old, he became the oldest Spurs player to feature in a League game. This record lasted until 2012, when it was beaten by goalkeeper Brad Friedel. Cantrell made 176 appearances and scored 84 goals for Spurs between 1912–1922. He formed part of the team that won the Second Division in 1920 and the FA Cup Final the following year.

22nd April 2017: Another classic FA Cup semi-final result for Spurs, who were defeated by Chelsea in a six-goal thriller at Wembley. Chelsea opened the scoring after five minutes but Harry Kane levelled with an instinctive stooping header, before Chelsea converted a penalty just before the break. In the second half, the match appeared very much in the balance, and Spurs quickly seemed to gain momentum, with Dele Alli converting Christian Eriksen's brilliant pass for an equaliser. But Chelsea scored again after 75 minutes to put them back ahead, before making it 4-2 five minutes later. It was an exciting game which ebbed and flowed all evening, and Spurs should be proud of their efforts. But the defeat was a depressing case of deja-vu for Tottenham, who had lost their past seven FA Cup semi-finals, more than any other club in the competition.

23rd April 1921: In an FA Cup Final played under hammering rain at Stamford Bridge, Tottenham beat Wolverhampton Wanderers 1-0 to earn our second FA Cup title. Jimmy Dimmock, who scored the winner, became the youngest Tottenham player to appear in an FA Cup Final, aged just 20 years and 139 days. The cup was presented by King George V. Manager Peter McWilliam became the first man to win the competition both as a player and as a manager.

24th April 1940: In an 'away' game against Arsenal at White Hart Lane, we beat Arsenal 4-2, with goals from Andrew Duncan, Johnny Morrison (2) and Ronnie Dix. During the War, League football was suspended and reinstated as two regional Wartime Leagues. With Highbury closed by the War Office, Tottenham offered Arsenal the use of White Hart Lane. Whilst this move may seem unthinkable today, Tottenham were actually reciprocating Arsenal's hospitality during the First World War, when we made Highbury our temporary home.

25th April 1987: In this First Division match against Oxford United at White Hart Lane, goals from Chris Waddle and Paul Allen saw us take an early lead. The game looked set to end with a 2-1 win, but in a moment of magic, Glenn Hoddle scored his last goal for Spurs in spectacular style. Hoddle picked the ball up in his own half, chipped it through the Oxford defence, and picked it up the other side before slotting home to win 3-1.

26th April 2017: In this game at Crystal Palace, Spurs struggled to break down the disciplined opposition, but Christian Eriksen's superb late long-range strike into the bottom corner was enough to secure a victory. This was our eighth consecutive league win, a streak that we had not achieved since 1960. The win put Tottenham up to 74 points, surpassing our previous 2013 record of 72 points.

27th April 1901: Following a 2-2 draw with Sheffield United in the initial game, the FA Cup Final went to a replay at Burnden Park, Bolton. John Cameron opened the scoring before the legendary centre forward Sandy Brown scored another two, becoming the first player to score in every round of the tournament. We won 3-1 to lift our first FA Cup trophy. With this win, Southern League Tottenham became the first and only non-Football League side to win the FA Cup.

28th April 1951: In our first season back in Division One after being promoted the previous summer, Tottenham became First Division champions for the first time, securing the title in this 1-0 home win against Sheffield Wednesday. Under manager Arthur Rowe, who pioneered the "push and run" style of play, the early 1950s were an exciting time for Tottenham. A full squad of Spurs legends played in this winning side that included Ted Ditchburn, Alf Ramsey, Arthur Willis, Harry Clarke, Bill Nicholson, Ronnie Burgess, Les Medley, Sonny Walters, Len Duquemin, Peter Murphy and Eddie Baily.

29th April 1978: The previous season, under new manager Keith Burkinshaw, Tottenham had been relegated for the first time in 26 years. And in this final match of our first season back in Division Two, three teams remained in contention for promotion to the First Division: Tottenham, Southampton and Brighton. The game was against Southampton and Spurs needed only one point to ensure promotion over Brighton. But so did Southampton. In the end, a mutually beneficial goalless draw saw both Spurs and Southampton promoted. Many Brighton fans have since called this conveniently goalless match a 'stitch-up'.

30th April 2017: Spurs marked the final north London derby at White Hart Lane with an impressive 2-0 win. After a goalless first half, the Spurs players emerged from the interval at full throttle, putting on a powerful but composed display that saw us overpower Arsenal. The opening goal came on 56 minutes when Dele Alli poked home from close range. Harry Kane then converted a penalty two minutes later, to score his 27th goal of the season. This was Spurs' ninth successive League win, our longest run since 1960, and also our 13th consecutive League victory at White Hart Lane. The win also ensured that we finished the season above Arsenal for the first time in 22 years.

May

1st May 2010: A nervous game for Spurs who were desperate to make a top-four finish for the first time in 20 years. And the players were probably still haunted by the memory of the last time they had found themselves so close to a Champions League finish, 4 years earlier, they had literally thrown up the chance when half the squad were struck down with food poisoning. With the prize so tantalisingly close, in this game against Bolton, the team were on edge until the final whistle, but Tom Huddlestone's thunderous first-half goal proved to be the winner. It wasn't the convincing win we'd hoped for, but Spurs pulled through to take them a step closer to Europe.

2nd May 2016: Spurs' only hope of claiming our first Premier League title since 1961 was to win the final three games of the season. Knowing nothing but a victory at Stamford Bridge would suffice, Spurs stormed into an early two-goal lead with goals from Harry Kane and Son Heung-min. But despite our heroic efforts, Chelsea left our Premier League title dreams in tatters, as they came back to secure a 2-2 draw. With frustration levels rising, tempers boiled over. Danny Rose and Willian had to be pulled apart by Mauricio Pochettino before Mousa Dembele appeared to gouge Diego Costa's eye. In this thrilling clash that became known as the "Battle of the Bridge", Spurs were shown an embarrassing Premier League record nine yellow cards. Ultimately the celebrations were only for Leicester who, with Spurs unable to win, were guaranteed the 2016 Premier League title.

3rd May 1972: A crowd of 38,362 packed into Molineux to witness the first leg of the first-ever UEFA Cup Final, played between Tottenham Hotspur and Wolverhampton Wanderers. Spurs had never lost a Cup Final and had no intention of breaking the spell. Goalkeeper Pat Jennings produced a series of outstanding saves and, after a goalless first half, Martin Chivers broke the stalemate with a powerful header. Wolves came back with an equaliser but, in another moment of magic, Chivers stunned the crowd by firing an unstoppable drive from 25 yards just three minutes from time, to hand Spurs a 2-1 first-leg victory. The second leg was played two weeks later on 17th May 1972...

4th May 2013: This Premier League game against Southampton at White Hart Lane was all about Gareth Bale, who scored the winning goal against his former club when he unleashed a tremendous low drive from 25 yards that flashed into the far corner, just four minutes from time. It was Bale's 200th appearance for Spurs, and his winning goal was his 20th League goal of the season, making him the first Spur to reach this landmark since Jurgen Klinsmann in 1994-95. It was also Bale's 8th goal scored from outside the box that season, more than any other player in the Premier League.

5th May 2010: In possibly the most important match of the Premier League era, Tottenham battled against Manchester City, in what was essentially a play-off for fourth place and entry into the Champions League. The three-point victory was worth a lot to both teams, both personally and financially. Spurs dominated throughout the match, but most of the game was spent on a nerve-wracking goalless knife edge. But Spurs held their nerve and, with only 8 minutes remaining, Peter Crouch headed home a dramatic late goal to earn Spurs a much deserved 1-0 victory and another 'glory, glory' night for the Club's history books. The result was a glowing tribute to the work of new manager Harry Redknapp, who had taken over only the previous season when Spurs were languishing in the relegation zone.

6th May 1961: 100,000 people crammed into Wembley to witness Spurs beat Leicester City 2-0, to win the 1961 FA Cup Final and complete the 1961 "Double", having also won the League Cup. The two goals were scored by Bobby Smith and Terry Dyson. The Double had not been achieved by any club in the 20th century, and not at all since Aston villa in 1897. The feat had often been regarded as an impossible task, but undeterred by such views, captain Danny Blanchflower had said in interviews earlier that season that that was exactly what Spurs intended to do.

7th May 2006: "Lasagne-gate"… a day no fan will ever forget. This was Spurs' biggest League fixtures for years; a win over West Ham would see us finish in 4th place ahead of Arsenal, and secure a spot in the UEFA Champions League for the first time. However, the drama began well before kick-off, as food poisoning dramatically struck down 10 of our players the night before, with rumours spreading that it was the result of a dodgy lasagne served up by a Hammers-supporting chef. Spurs manager Martin Jol put in a request to have the game postponed, but this was rejected. Unsurprisingly, the peaky Spurs players did not start well, falling behind after ten minutes. They bravely battled back and got themselves in front just after the half-hour mark, but West Ham came back to defeat us 2-1, leaving Tottenham's Champions League dreams in tatters.

8th May 2019: Spurs beat Ajax in the UEFA Champions League Semi-Final, to gain entry to our first ever Champions League Final. Trailing 1-0 from the first leg, Spurs made the worst possible start in Amsterdam when a fifth-minute header by Ajax doubled their advantage. Then Ajax scored again, leaving Spurs down 3-0 on aggregate. Yet in another pulsating semi-final, Mauricio Pochettino's side scored twice within five minutes in the second half. And in a frantic finish, Lucas Moura completed his hat-trick deep into injury-time, with a left-foot shot from 16 yards, to pull Spurs back to

3-3 in an astonishing comeback. Tottenham won on away goals to reach an all-English Champions League final against Liverpool in Madrid. And sadly we all know the rest.

9th May 1981: In the 100th FA Cup Final, and Spurs' first in 14 years, we drew 1-1 with Manchester City at Wembley. Manchester City opened the scoring in the 30th minute but scored an own-goal in the 79th minute to bring Spurs level. The replay, perhaps one of the greatest Spurs matches of all time, took place five days later ...

10th May 1982: Goalkeeper Tony Parks made his Spurs debut in a 2-2 draw with West Ham at Upton Park. Our goals were scored by Gary Brooke and Glenn Hoddle. Parks made fewer than 50 appearances for Spurs, but he is best remembered for his heroic performance in the 1984 UEFA Cup Final, where he made the deciding save of a dramatic penalty shootout.

11th May 2014: In Tim Sherwood's last game as manager before being sacked, a comfortable 3-0 victory over Aston Villa secured us a place in the Europa League. Paulinho hit home the first after cutting through the heart of the Villa defence to collect Gylfi Sigurdsson's pass. Aston Villa then helpfully headed in an own goal before Emmanuel Adebayor converted a penalty to make it 3-0. The win meant that Sherwood finished his reign having won 59% of games, better than any Spurs manager in Premier League history.

12th May 2019: An entertaining 2-2 draw with Everton earnt Spurs the point we needed to finish fourth in the League and secure a place in the Champions League for a fourth successive season. In the game at White Hart Lane, Eric Dier quickly slammed us in front after three minutes. Everton came back with two quick-fire goals in the second half, but Christian Eriksen earnt us the point we needed with a rasping low free-kick for a 2-2 draw. Despite a rocky start to the season, Spurs had finished on a high, and Pochettino called it the best season at the club.

13th May 2017: In the perfect send-off to 118 years at White Hart Lane, Tottenham gave the ground a finale it deserved with a 2-1 victory over Manchester United. The atmosphere was electric; flags fluttering in the crowd, the rain pouring down, and former heroes returning for the celebration. Victor Wanyama got Spurs off to the best possible start with a powerful header after just five minutes. Kane doubled the lead early in the second half, flicking home from a Christian Eriksen free-kick. And in another tribute to the stadium, with the win completed Spurs' season of unbeaten home games at the Lane.

14th May 1981: Following a 1-1 draw with Manchester City five days earlier, the FA Cup Final went to a replay. It was the 100th Final of the FA Cup and our first for 14 years. Ricky Villa shrugged off his disappointment of being substituted in the initial match when he opened the scoring in the 8th minute. But City equalised 3 minutes later and then converted a penalty just after the interval to put them ahead. In the 70th minute, a goal from Garth Crooks brought the score up to 2-2. Then, in a moment of dramatic excitement, Ricky Villa picked up the ball on the left touchline, dribbled towards goal, skipping past four City defenders, before scoring the most famous FA Cup Final goal of all time. The brilliant goal was later recognised with the Wembley Goal of the Century award in 2001.

15th May 1963: Spurs became the first British club to lift a European trophy, when they won the 1963 European Cup Winners' Cup, hammering defending champions Atletico Madrid 5-1 in the Final in Rotterdam. The Spurs goals were scored by Jimmy Greaves (2), John White and Terry Dyson (2). Spurs legend Jimmy Greaves became the club's highest League goalscorer in one season with 37 goals.

16th May 2009: In the final home game of the season, a 2-1 victory over Manchester City saw Tottenham finish with a flourish. Spurs took the lead after 28 minutes when Jermain Defoe swooped in front of the City defence to steer the ball into the net with an audacious back-heeled opener. City equalised after the break, but Keane scored a late winner from a penalty after City brought down Fraizer Campbell. Spurs set a new club record for conceding just ten home goals in the whole season and also conceded fewer goals than any other Premier League club that season.

17th May 1972: In the first all-English European final, Tottenham beat Wolverhampton Wanderers to win the first-ever UEFA Cup competition, which had replaced the Inter-Cities Fairs Cup. Following our 2-1 win in the first leg, Spurs started with a one-goal advantage. In the 29th minute, captain Alan Mullery threw himself head-first into the ball to add another goal for Spurs and beat Wolves 3-2 on aggregate. Alan Mullery lifted the trophy and to mark his final competitive game for Spurs, he completed a lap of honour to the cheers of jubilant fans. This was Tottenham's second European trophy, making them the first British club to achieve the feat.

18th May 2017: Spurs inflicted their biggest ever away win in the Premier League, crushing the reigning champions, Leicester City, 6-1. Despite Chelsea ending our Premier League title hopes the previous week, there was no let-up from Mauricio Pochettino's side. Spurs were exceptional and no one was better than Harry Kane, who scored four times in another superb performance. Son Heung-min also scored either side of half-time, volleying in Dele Alli's masterful pass and bending in another from 25 yards.

19th May 2013: During a match against Sunderland, news began to spread through the stadium that Spurs had been thwarted by Arsenal in the chase for fourth place. In any other game, a stunning

90th-minute winner from Gareth Bale would have sent the crowd wild but where there would usually be elation, there was only deflation. Nothing could lift our spirits as our Champions League hopes lay in tatters. Forced smiles for this hollow victory were unable to mask the utter dejection felt by the players and fans alike.

20th May 1967: "Cockney Cup Final". The FA Cup Final between Tottenham and Chelsea at Wembley Stadium was the first FA Cup Final to be contested between two London teams. Spurs won the match 2-1, thanks to goals from Jimmy Robertson and Frank Saul.

21st May 2017: In our biggest ever away win, Spurs thrashed already-relegated Hull City 7-1 at the KCOM Stadium. Two goals from Harry Kane and another from Dele Alli put us up 3-0 by half time. Then after the break, Victor Wanyama headed in to cancel out Hull's consolatory effort, before the prolific Kane got his third. Two late goals from defenders Ben Davies and Toby Alderweireld made sure Hull exited the Premier League with a whimper. Harry Kane's hat-trick was his fifth of the season, and secured him the Premier League golden boot for the second year in a row, the first English player to achieve this feat since Michael Owen 18 years earlier.

22nd May 1982: FA Cup Final between Tottenham and Queens Park Rangers at Wembley Stadium. Spurs were having a strong season, and at one point, had been campaigning for silverware on four fronts; we had reached both the League Cup Final (but lost to Liverpool after extra time) and the semi-finals of the European Cup Winners' Cup (but were beaten by Barcelona), and also finished 4th in the League. This FA Cup Final was our last chance of a trophy. Spurs were the better team, being matched against Second Division QPR, but we were missing two of our best players, Ossie Ardiles and Ricky Villa. Ardiles had returned home to Argentina to prepare for the World Cup Final, whilst Villa was omitted because of the on-going hostilities with

Argentina during the Falklands War. A goalless game went into extra time and in the 109th minute Glenn Hoddle struck, but QPR equalised to leave the final score at 1-1. The Final went to a replay 5 days later....

23rd May 1984: In perhaps the greatest night White Hart Lane has witnessed, Spurs won the 2nd leg of the UEFA Cup Final against defending Champions RSC Anderlecht of Belgium. Anderlecht took the lead but with time running out, Graham Roberts grabbed the precious equaliser. The game went to extra time but the score remained 2–2 on aggregate, forcing a penalty shoot-out. Danny Thomas missed his spot kick but it didn't matter, as man-of-the-moment Tony Parks heroically saved two Anderlecht penalties, helping Spurs to a 4–3 victory on a night that will forever hold him in the affections of Spurs fans.

24th May 2015: A confident 1-0 win over Everton at Goodison Park saw Spurs finish 5th in the Premier League and qualify for the group stage of the Europa League. Harry Kane scored a precise first-half header, his 21st Premier League goal of the season. Spurs had previously only ever seen three other players score more than 20 goals in a season: Gareth Bale (2012/13), Jurgen Klinsmann (1994/95) and Teddy Sheringham (1992/93). And, impressively, this would be only Kane's first of four consecutive seasons in which he would achieve the feat.

25th May 2007: Gareth Bale signed from Southampton for an initial transfer fee of £5 million, with potential to rise to £10 million. In the six years at Tottenham, Bale's exceptional play saw him rise to international stardom. He was named PFA Players' Player of the Year in 2011 and 2013 and, also in 2013, was named PFA Young Player of the Year, the FWA Footballer of the Year and the Premier League Player of the Season. He was named in the PFA Team of the Year for three consecutive years 2011, 2012 and 2013. In 2013, Tottenham sold Bale to Real Madrid for a world record £85 million, making him the most expensive player in the world.

26th May 1907: In the second and final fixture on our tour of Belgium, Spurs beat Ostend 8-1 at Union St Gilloise. Max Seeburg bagged a hat-trick, with the other goals scored by Woodward (2), Payne (2) and Whyman.

27th May 1982: FA Cup Final replay against QPR at Wembley Stadium following a draw 5 days earlier. It had been a long and tiring season, and at one point, Spurs had been campaigning for silverware on four fronts; we had reached both the League Cup Final and the semi-finals of the European Cup Winners' Cup, and also finished 4th in the League. The FA Cup Final was the last chance of being rewarded for all the hard work. Glenn Hoddle scored an early penalty after 6 minutes, that sent the goalkeeper diving the wrong way. But as the match continued, the players' fatigue was beginning to show. In the second half, the Spurs defence was under constant pressure as QPR put everything into getting an equaliser. There were many close calls but Spurs managed to hold out to retain the FA Cup Title and lift our seventh FA Cup.

28th May 1952: Our best ever scoreline was an 18-1 win over Saskatchewan FA XI at Saskatoon on tour in Canadian. Sid McClellan netted nine of the goals. Spurs were up 14-0 at half-time, before the teams swapped goalkeepers and Ted Ditchburn's strong display ensured that Spurs only scored another four.

29th May 1984: A testimonial match for Keith Burkinhaw at White Hart Lane ended in a 2-2 draw with an England XI. The Spurs goals were scored by Chris Hughton and Gary Brady. Burkinshaw managed the club between 1976 and 1984 and is remembered as one of Spurs' greatest managers, guiding us to FA Cup success in 1981 and 1982, as well as the UEFA Cup in 1984. He won more major football competitions for the club than any other Spurs manager, apart from Bill Nicholson.

30th May 1983: Garth Crooks scored all three of our goals in a 3-2 friendly victory at Alesund in Norway.

31st May 1984: Keith Burkinshaw left as manager after eight years with the club. In a disappointing first season in charge, Burkinshaw saw Spurs relegated for the first time in 26 years, but the club allowed him to stay and he rewarded their faith by restoring Spurs to the top flight the following season. Burkinshaw went on to guide the club to two successive FA Cup titles in 1981 and 1982, and to the 1984 UEFA Cup title for a second time. Burkinshaw is remembered as one of Spurs' greatest managers, winning more major football competitions at the club than any other Spurs manager, apart from Bill Nicholson.

June

1st June 1959: On tour in the USSR, we beat Dynamo Kyiv 2-1, with both goals scored by Johnny Brooks. The tour has since been credited as a key event that brought together the successful team of the early 1960s that achieved the famous "Double" in 1961. Dave Mackay later said, "I shall always believe we laid the foundations of the team-spirit and genuine friendship which has since played a notable part in the success of Tottenham Hotspur Football Club". The party notably included future legends Danny Blanchflower, Dave Mackay, Terry Medwin, Bobby Smith and Cliff Jones.

2nd June 1952: On tour in Canada we beat Victoria and District 7-0 with Eddie Baily scoring four of the goals. We played eight further matches in Canada on the tour, winning all nine games and scoring an incredible total of 78 goals. This included an 18-1 victory over Saskatchewan FA and a 5-0 win against Manchester United in Toronto.

3rd June 2004: Jacques Santini took over as manager, but his reign was short, announcing his resignation after just 13 games. Officially, Santini left due to personal problems, but it was widely reported that his departure was a result of a series of disagreements with the then Sporting Director, Frank Arnesen.

4th June 1979: Captain Steve Perryman lifted the Japan Cup following a 2-0 victory over Dundee United at National Stadium in Tokyo. The goals were scored by Gordon Smith and Osvaldo Ardiles.

5th June 1909: During the summer of 1909 we travelled with Everton to South America for a seven-match tour of Argentina and Uruguay. In this first game in Palermo, goals by Walter Tull and Bert Middlemiss saw us draw 2-2 with Everton. On the way back from the tour, we famously returned with a parrot, apparently a gift from the ship's captain. In an uncanny coincidence, the parrot died on the same day that Spurs were unfairly relegated in favour of corrupt Arsenal during the expansion of the First Division. Supposedly, this is the origin of the phrase "as sick as a parrot".

6th June 1979: On the way back from winning the Japan Cup, we defeated a Bermuda Select XI 3-1 in Hamilton. A depleted squad meant that the club's secretary and physiotherapist had to play.

7th June 1947: In June 1947, the League was still ongoing due to severe weather the previous winter and government restrictions on midweek fixtures. In our latest finish to a season, Spurs played Barnsley and drew 1-1. Ronnie Dix scored from a penalty. Of course, the 2019-20 season, suspended due to the Covid-19 outbreak, ran on into an even later finish.

8th June 1938: Legendary goalkeeper Ted Ditchburn signed as an amateur for the club. A good class boxer as a schoolboy, Ditchburn was highly regarded for his athleticism and strength. He made a club record 452 appearances for Spurs, a record that remained until 1975. He played in an unbroken run of 247 matches between April 1948 and March 1954, and was an ever-present member of the famous 'push and run' of the early 1950s. A broken finger against Chelsea ended his career in 1958.

9th June 2015: Amid speculation that he would be joining Manchester United, Christian Eriksen confirmed to Danish media that he would stay at Tottenham for the foreseeable future, saying, "I feel right at home at Tottenham". And he did stay, until he signed for Inter Milan in January 2020. During his successful seven years with Spurs, he became only the second player after David Beckham to record more than ten assists in four successive Premier League seasons.

10th June 2001: Gus Poyet signed from Chelsea for £2.2 million. In his debut season, he scored 14 goals and helped his team reach the League Cup Final. Poyet remained at Spurs for the rest of his career, making a total of 98 appearances and scoring 23 goals.

11th June 1983: In our second match against Manchester United in the Swazispa International Challenge Cup in Swaziland, we won 2-0 thanks to goals from Steve Perryman and Gary Mabbutt. In a third match, we joined forces with United to form a 'Tottman' XI that thrashed Swaziland 6-1.

12th June 1966: On tour in Mexico, Spurs beat the Mexican National team 1-0 with a late goal from Alan Gilzean. Although only a friendly, in light of the upcoming World Cup, the match was highly anticipated and attracted a crowd of 100,000. Just over a month later, the England team would meet the very same Mexico National side in the group stages of the World Cup.

13th June 2012: Harry Redknapp was sacked as manager after an entertaining four years at Spurs. After inheriting a struggling club in 2008, Redknapp had had an immediate galvanising effect on the players, leading the club to two fourth-place finishes in three years. His success as a manager was based mainly on his skill of motivation and stirring up passion, rather than on tactics, but he became hugely popular with fans and players alike. With 236 Premier League wins as manager, he is one of only four managers to have won over 200 Premier League games. As Tottenham began to climb up the League, Redknapp began to receive international acclaim, and by 2012 was tipped as top favourite to take over as England manager. But the stardom and celebrity appeared to be Redknapp's downfall. The promise of the England job distracted Redknapp from his current role and he took his eye off the ball. Spurs did manage to finish fourth that season, but it was a far cry from the 1st place that Redknapp had looked set to deliver in the New Year. The board were unimpressed and dismissed Redknapp from the club.

14th June 1994: As punishment for financial irregularities committed under the club's previous ownership, the FA penalised Tottenham with a record £600,000 fine, a 12 point deduction, and a suspension from the 1994-95 FA Cup. The investigation covered 40 charges of malpractice relating to the purchase of 15 players in the 1980s. The harsh punishment effectively amounted to relegation by a slow and painful process. Fans were devastated but chairman Alan Sugar was furious; not only was the malpractice was historical but it had been the club themselves who had identified and reported the issue to the FA. Alan Sugar immediately ordered an appeal.

15th June 1952: Whilst on tour in Toronto, we hammered Manchester United 7-1, having also beaten them 5-0 the day before.

16th June 1974: Alan Gilzean scored three in our 6-0 victory over a Mauritius Select XI in Curepipe. The other three goals came from Ralph Coates, Steve Perryman and Martin Peters. During the tour, we played the Mauritius select XI on another two occasions, inflicting heavy thrashings in all three matches.

17th June 1966: During our tour of Bermuda, the USA and Mexico, we defeated Bayern Munich 3-0 in Detroit, thanks to goals from Keith Weller, Frank Saul and Terry Venables. The two teams met again just 2 days later in Chicago, where we drew 1-1.

18th June 1952: During a 10-match tour in Canada, we thrashed a Quebec FA XI 8-0 in Montreal, bringing our total tour goals to an incredible 85. Sid McClennan and Les Bennett both scored hat-tricks.

19th June 2020: Not since the War has the Football League been put on hold, but in unprecedented circumstances, all fixtures were suspended due to the global COVID-19 pandemic. As restrictions on 'social distancing' eased, the FA scrambled to restart the season, planning 26 games in just 16 days. In their first match in three months, Spurs played Manchester United at the new Tottenham Hotspur Stadium. Playing behind closed doors, the sounds of cheering crowds and team chants were pumped into the deserted stadium. January signing Steven Bergwijn scored the opener when he picked up the ball 35 yards out and made a surging run through the defence, before smashing in a powerful shot that the United keeper could only parry into the roof of the net. We came close to grabbing a second when Bergwijn delivered a well-placed cross met by Son, who arrowed a powerful header towards the top corner, which was superbly saved. And United equalised with a penalty in the 81st minute. It was a frustrating first game back for Spurs, who needed the points, and the draw left us sitting in eighth place.

20th June 2016: A goalless draw for England with Slovakia in Saint-Etienne in France saw them qualify for the knockout stages of Euro 2016. The Spurs players were in the thick of the action, with Eric Dier, Dele Alli and Harry Kane all attacking well, while Danny Rose and Kyle Walker were on the bench. Eric tried some long-range shots, Dele saw an angled effort cleared off the line just seconds after coming off the bench, and Kane saw a couple of difficult headers loop off target. Tottenham have provided 78 international players to the England team over the years, more than any other club.

21st June 1989: Gary Lineker signed from Barcelona for £1.1 million. In his 138 games for Spurs, Lineker scored 80 goals, finishing as top scorer in the First Division in 1989–90 and second-top in 1991-92 behind Ian Wright. Lineker was also part of the successful Spurs team that won the 1991 FA Cup Final. In 1992, he won the FWA Footballer of the Year, before transferring to Nagoya Grampus Eight.

22nd June 1991: Alan Sugar joined the directorate and rescued the club from impending bankruptcy. Alan Sugar later described his time at Tottenham as "a waste of my life". Sorry about that Alan. Just for the record, the club is now estimated to be worth around £1.3 billion.

23rd June 2020: In a frenzy of catch-up matches after the season was suspended due to the Covid-19 pandemic, Spurs faced West Ham at the Tottenham Hotspur Stadium. After Son Heung-Min was denied a goal by VAR, a West Ham own-goal on 64 minutes finally gifted Spurs the breakthrough we deserved. Then, eight minutes from time, Harry Kane raced onto Son's through-ball to strike in the winner. This was Kane's 30th goal in a London Derby, with only Teddy Sheringham, Frank Lampard and Thierry Henry having netted more. It was also Kane's 200th Premier League appearance for Spurs, and his 137 goals in this time are bettered only by Sergio Aguero who scored 138 goals in his first 200 Premier League games for Manchester City.

24th June 1965: On tour in Israel, we beat a Maccabi Select XI 3-2 in Tel Aviv. The goals were scored by Alan Mullery, Dave Mackay and Alan Gilzean. This was the final match of the tour, which was played for the John White Cup, a trophy offered by the Israeli side in memory of the legendary Spurs player John White who had been tragically killed by lightning the previous summer.

25th June 1950: Full back Alf Ramsey became the first Spur to feature in a World Cup match when we beat Chile 2-0 in Rio de Janeiro. Then in the next game against Spain, Eddie Baily also made his England debut. Ramsey had been signed by Spurs the previous year for a then club-record fee of £21,000, and quickly became a cornerstone of Arthur Rowe's famous 'push and run' side. When later talking about the 1949-50 season, Rowe said, "as much as anything else, I would rate our good time last year to the acquisition of Alf Ramsey".

26th June 1998: In a World Cup qualifying game in France, England defeated Columbia 2-0. Despite recurrent injuries during the season earning him the nickname "Sicknote" amongst Spurs fans, Darren Anderton was given a chance by England manager, Glenn Hoddle. Anderton rewarded Hoddle's faith when he scored the first goal of the match, to help England qualify for the knock-out stages of the competition.

27th June 2008: Brazil international goalkeeper Heurelho Gomes was signed from PSV Eindhoven by new manager Juande Ramos for a reported £7.8 million transfer fee. Gomes was our top-choice goalkeeper for several years but after a series of high-profile errors, he was replaced by 40-year-old Brad Friedel and then France international Hugo Lloris, relegating Gomes down to third-choice.

28th June 1941: Spurs winger Bert Middlemiss died in Brixham. He featured in our first League match in 1908 and in the following 11 years, went on to score 55 goals in a total of 261 matches.

29th June 1908: After several failed attempts we gained entry to the Football League. We were competing with Lincoln City to be elected into the League, but the League Management Committee voted 5-3 in our favour. We entered the Second Division alongside Bradford Park Avenue, replacing Lincoln City and Stoke. In our first season in the Football League, Tottenham finished in second place, earning immediate promotion to the First Division.

30th June 1995: Chris Armstrong transferred from Crystal Palace for a then club-record £4.5 million. Earlier that year, Armstrong became the first Premier League player to receive a doping ban, and following his slow start for Spurs, he was criticised by tabloids as an inadequate replacement for Jürgen Klinsmann. However, he built up a prolific partnership with Teddy Sheringham and went on to score 48 goals in 141 Premier League appearances and was part of the successful team that won the 1999 League Cup.

July

1st July 1969: Full-back Terry Naylor signed for Tottenham. His tough style of play, and his background as a meat porter at London's Smithfield Market, earned him the nickname "Meathook". In his 11 years at the club, Naylor made 314 appearances for Spurs and featured in the 1974 UEFA Cup Final against Feyenoord.

2nd July 2019: Tottenham signed Tanguy Ndombele in a deal worth £55.45 million, far surpassing the previous £42m club record fee paid for Davinson Sanchez in 2017. Within a minute of coming off the bench in his debut against Juventus, Ndombele assisted Lucas Moura, helping Tottenham to a 3-2 win in the 2019 International Champions Cup .

3rd July 2012: Andre Villas-Boas was appointed Head Coach following the dismissal of Harry Redknapp. Despite having never played football professionally himself, AVB was a hugely successful manager for Spurs. By the new year, the club had risen to third place in the League and, in February 2013, he guided Tottenham to the last 16 of the UEFA Europa League. He won the Manager of the Month award for December 2012 and February 2013 and finished his first season in charge with a club record 72 points, the most points ever scored by a Premier League club not to finish in the top four. Under AVB, 59% of Premier League games finished in a win, more than any other Spurs manager.

4th July 2012: New manager Andre Villas-Boas made his first signing for Spurs when he bought Icelandic international Gylfi Sigurdsson from 1899 Hoffenheim. Gylfi was an instant success and, the following

January, Reading made three unsuccessful bids to buy Gylfi back, including a club-record offer of around £10 million. After only two years at Spurs, Gylfi rejoined another of his former clubs, Swansea City.

5th July 2007: Younes Kaboul signed from French team Auxerre for an undisclosed fee believed to be around £8 million. Kaboul was immediately popular with fans and was admired for his power and aggression on the pitch. Kaboul went on to make 29 appearances for Spurs and was part of the team that won the 2008 League Cup. He transferred to Portsmouth in 2008 before returning to Spurs 18 months later for a reported £9.5 million. On being asked about resigning Kaboul, manager Harry Redknapp said that Kaboul was "much improved" and was a "late developer".

6th July 1993: Former captain and Spurs legend Steve Perryman was appointed assistant manager by new boss Ossie Ardiles. Perryman was one of Spurs' greatest ever players, making a club record 800 appearances, including 656 League games. He won the UEFA Cup in 1972 and 1984, the FA Cup in 1981 and 1982, and the League Cup in 1971 and 1973.

7th July 1988: Paul Gascoigne transferred from Newcastle for a reported £2 million. In his four years at Tottenham, Gazza made 112 appearances, scoring 33 goals. In 1990, he was named as BBC Sports Personality of the Year and Tottenham Hotspur's Player of the Year, and was named on the PFA Team of the Year in 1991. Despite winning the 1991 FA Cup, the Final ended in disaster for Paul Gascoigne, when he committed a dangerous knee-high foul, rupturing his cruciate ligaments in his right knee. With the club drowning in debt and close to bankruptcy, Spurs hired a financial advisor who suggested selling the injured Gascoigne to Lazio. Many people believed that Gazza had the potential to have become the best player in the world, and news of his potential transfer dominated the tabloids for months, often overshadowing other serious political events of the time, such as the heavy financial recession.

8th July 1980: Robbie Keane born in Dublin. By the time he joined Spurs in 2002, he was already an established Irish international. In two separate spells at the club, Keane scored 122 goals in 306 appearances. In his first season, he finished as Tottenham's top scorer with 13 goals. In the 2007–08 season, Keane scored a personal record of 23 goals, including a landmark 100th competitive goal, and won his first League Cup.

9th July 1918: Spurs player Finlay Weir was killed in action in WW1 whilst serving with the Tottenham Royal Engineers. After moving to the club in May 1912, Weir made 101 appearances and scored two goals over the course of the following three seasons, before competitive football was suspended due to the outbreak of War. There were around 5000 professional footballers at the start of the First World War, and it is thought that 2000 of them signed up, with a number of them joining the 'Football Battalion'. Sadly, many of them were killed, paying the ultimate sacrifice for their country. The other Tottenham players who lost their lives in the War were John Fleming, John Jarvie, Alf Hobday, John Hebdon, Ed Lightfoot, William Lloyd, Alexander MacGregor, Archie Wilson, Norman Wood and Walter Tull.

10th July 1978: Spurs hit the headlines when we signed two stars of the successful Argentinian World Cup team, Ossie Ardiles and Ricardo Villa. It was big news, not only because of the international celebrity of the players but also because it marked the end of a 50-year ban on foreign players in the English Football League.

11th July 1966: Jimmy Greaves appeared in England's opening game of the 1966 World Cup at Wembley Stadium, a goalless draw with

Uruguay. At the time, Greaves was the leading goalscorer in the country and remains Spurs' best-ever goal-scorer, with 266 goals in his 379 appearances for the club. But despite his reputation, Greaves failed to score in any of the World Cup group stage matches. In the final group match against France, Greaves sustained a leg injury and was unable to play in the knock-out stages. He was fit to play in the Final, but manager Alf Ramsey left him out the team who had made it this far without him. It was a devastating blow to Greaves, who never returned to the mighty player he once was and retired prematurely in 1971.

12th July 2012: Belgian defender Jan Vertonghen joined Spurs from Ajax for £12.5million. Vertonghen went on to make over 200 appearances for the club, winning the player of the year award in 2018.

13th July 1944: Spurs' greatest left-back, Cyril Knowles, was born. A stalwart of the Spurs first team, he made 506 appearances during his 11 years at the club and missed only one league match between 1965 and 1969. Knowles won the FA Cup in 1967, the League Cup in 1971 and 1973 and the UEFA Cup in 1972. He also gained four caps for England. He was the inspiration for the pop song "Nice One Cyril" that was released by 'Cockerel Chorus' before the 1973 League Cup and peaked at number 14 in the UK singles charts after Tottenham won the title.

14th July 1976: Keith Burkinshaw succeeded Terry Neill as manager. In his first season in charge, Spurs were relegated for the first time in 26 years, but the club let him stay and their faith was rewarded when Burkinshaw immediately restored the club to the First Division. He went on to guide Spurs to FA Cup success in 1981 and 1982, as well as the UEFA Cup in 1984. He won more major football competitions for the club than any other Spurs manager, apart from Bill Nicholson.

15th July 1898: The Weekly Herald reported that "The Spurs will this year wear the colours of snow white shirts and navy blue knickers". This was in contrast to the orange-striped shirts worn in the previous two seasons and the red shirt worn before that. The traditional blue and white strip, in various forms, has continued to be worn ever since. The cockerel was added in 1921.

16th July 1984: Irving Scholar took over as chairman. Scholar was a lifelong Tottenham supporter and willingly took over a club struggling with debts of nearly £5 million, more than any English football at the time. Scholar significantly commercialised the club, diversifying into other areas, including computing, clothing and merchandise. He also floated the club on the London Stock Exchange, the first sports club in the world to do so. Scholar was one of the key figures who pushed for the formation of the more financially-lucrative Premier League.

17th July 1999: Steffen Iversen bagged a hat-trick and Jose Dominguez scored twice as we thrashed part-time club Lysekils 7-1 in a pre-season friendly in Sweden. Spurs were already 4-0 up at half-time, with goals from Campbell, Iversen (2) and Dominguez. After the break, Dominguez got his second on the hour, before Steve Carr smashed home two minutes later. Lysekil then pulled one back before Iversen completed his hat-trick.

18th July 1997: David Ginola made his Spurs debut on tour in Norway, two days after being signed by manager Gerry Francis. His compelling attacking skills and extravagant personality made him popular amongst fans. Ginola was named as both PFA Players' Player of the Year and FWA Footballer of the Year and became the first player in history to win the latter whilst at a club who finished the season outside of the top four.

19th July 2012: Ledley King announced he would retire from football after spending his entire career at Spurs. In his 13 years with the club, he made 323 appearances in all competitions. He received only eight yellow cards in his career, and Thierry Henry later stated that King was the best defender he had played against and the only one to tackle him without resorting to fouling.

20th July 1909: Walter Tull signed to Spurs for a fee of £10. Tull was only the second black professional footballer in the world after Arthur Wharton and the first to play in the top division. He made just 10 appearances before being dropped to the reserves. This may have been due to the appalling racial abuse he received from opposing fans, particularly at Bristol City. At the outbreak of the First World War, Tull enlisted in the war effort, becoming the first black officer in the British Army. At the age of just 29, Tull was tragically killed in action during the Spring Offensive of 1918. His body was never recovered. His death received little media attention and it is only in recent years that his story has started to be fully recognised. There have been repeated appeals for Tull to be posthumously awarded the Military Cross, something which he was denied at the time due to his skin colour.

21st July 1964: Scottish international John White was tragically killed by lightning whilst playing golf, aged just 27. White had been signed by Bill Nicholson in 1959 and was a cornerstone of Spurs' Double winning team of 1961. He was highly regarded for his excellent passing, tight ball control and speedy runs that would see him arrive unexpectedly in the penalty area and earned him the nickname "The Ghost". With White on the team, Tottenham never finished worse than fourth place in the First Division and, of the 15 matches he missed, Tottenham only won one. Cliff Jones later described White as "a great talent... John White would bring himself into a game... He was always available if you needed to pass to someone".

22nd July 2003: In a pre-season match at Norwich, an enthusiastic home side pushed hard from the start, with Spurs only just able to hold them off. As the game progressed, Spurs found their feet to secure a comfortable 3-0 win. The pre-season spotlight has been focused on new striker Bobby Zamora, who did score one of the goals, but midfielder Darren Anderton stole the show with a magnificent 25-yard curling strike, his first goal for over a year due to recurrent injuries. Simon Davies scored the other goal.

23rd July 2017: Spurs faced Paris Saint-Germain in a pre-season International Champions Cup clash in Orlando. PSG dominated from the off and Spurs fell behind after less than 6 minutes. But both teams continued to play a very open game, and in a moment of magic, Christian Eriksen brought Spurs level, when he unleashed a dipping drive from 30 yards on 11 minutes, and Spurs then took the lead with an unconventional goal from Eric Dier minutes later. PSG equalised before the break, but Spurs ran out winners with two late goals from Toby Alderweireld and Harry Kane, as we impressed the crowd in Orlando. To add further excitement to the already eventful night, PSG's German international goalkeeper Kevin Trapp was also shown a red card for a deliberate handball outside his penalty area.

24th July 2005: In the 2005 Peace Cup Final at Seoul World Cup Stadium in South Korea, Spurs defeated Olympique Lyonnais 3–1 to win the Peace Cup.

25th July 2007: Danny Rose was signed from Leeds for a transfer fee of around £1 million. At the time, Leeds had been struggling with financial difficulties and were forced to sell off many of their players. Rose had to wait almost three years before making his league debut, but when he did, he made quite the stir. In his debut against Arsenal, Rose scored the first goal of the match after just ten minutes, which was later described by The Times as "a volley so thunderous that you could hear the whack off his boot above the din of the raucous crowd". It went on to win Goal of the Season. Danny Rose is the longest-serving current Spurs player.

26th July 1988: On tour in Sweden, Paul Stewart and Paul Gascoigne made their Spurs debuts as we beat Vederslov 4-1. Paul Stewart had been signed for £1.7 million from Manchester City, becoming the first Spurs player costing over £1 million and the most expensive player ever in the Second Division.

27th July 2009: Peter Crouch returned to Spurs for a second stint, transferring from Portsmouth for a fee of £10 million. Crouch had initially signed for Spurs in 1998, but he did not make any appearances for their first team before being sold to QPR in 2000. Following his return, Crouch scored 24 goals and provided 21 assists in his two-year stay at Spurs, before being swapped out in favour of on-loaner striker Emmanuel Adebayor.

28th July 1993: Spurs legend Harry Kane was born in Walthamstow. After coming up through Spurs' youth academy, Kane joined the senior team at just 16. In his first full season at the club, he finished as the second-highest goalscorer in the Premier League, before quickly becoming the League's top goal-scorer for the following two seasons. In the 2017–18 season, Kane scored an incredible 41 goals in 48 games in all competitions and, in November 2019, became Tottenham's third-highest goalscorer ever behind Jimmy Greaves and Bobby Smith. Kane has won the Premier League Player of the Month awards six times, once less than record-holder Sergio Aguero. In his first 200 Premier League appearance for Tottenham, Kane scored 137 goals, again only bettered only by Manchester City's Sergio Aguero who scored 138.

29th July 1994: Tottenham signed German international Jurgen Klinsmann from Monaco for £2 million the day before his 30th birthday. Klinsmann was already internationally renowned, having been part of the successful German team that won the 1990 World Cup and had recently made the quarter-finals in 1994. The signing resembled that of Ossie Ardiles and Ricky Villa in 1978 who arrived straight from the successful Argentinian World Cup team. Chairman Alan Sugar hoped the high-profile signing would boost morale in the club, which had recently been heavily penalised for historical financial irregularities.

30th July 1984: This was the last game in our three-match tour of Sweden and Norway, where we won all three matches.

31st July 2009: In this match against Hull City at the Beijing Workers Stadium, Spurs won the Premier League Asia Trophy for the fourth time. Captain Robbie Keane scored two in our 3–0 win. The competition was a knockout tournament between four teams: Hull City, Tottenham Hotspur, West Ham United and Beijing Guoan. Questions were raised when, just two weeks before the final, only 20,000 of the 120,000 tickets had been sold. It transpired that ticket sales had been hampered by the spreading rumours that Beijing Guoan would only be fielding a second-team side in order to rest their best players for the upcoming China Super League match.

August

1st August 1987: On tour in Sweden and Finland, we beat the Lansi Uudenmaan XI 7-2 at Karjala. Shaun Close scored four, Clive Allen bagged a brace and Chris Fairclough scored the other. This was our first ever match in Finland.

2nd August 2014: Eric Dier signed for Spurs in a £4 million transfer deal. He made his arrival known, scoring the only goal in his debut match against West Ham on the first day of the new season. Dier has made over 200 appearances for Tottenham and was part of the team that played in the 2015 Football League Cup Final and the 2019 UEFA Champions League Final.

3rd August 2010: After being invited by Benfica to play in the Eusebio Cup in Lisbon, we beat the hosts 1-0 thanks to a second-half goal from Gareth Bale. The Eusébio Cup is an annual two-team pre-season friendly hosted by Benfica at the Estádio da Luz in Lisbon. The glass trophy is dedicated to the late Benfica player and footballing legend Eusébio, who was the highest goalscorer in the 1966 World Cup.

4th August 1984: Two of the heroes of the triumphant 1978 Argentinian World Cup team, Ossie Ardiles and Mario Kempes, played alongside each other for Spurs in a pre-season friendly against Enfield. We won 7-0, with Garth Crooks scoring four. Ardiles was already an established Spurs player and striker Mario Kempes was on trial attempting to earn a contract. He was not taken on.

5th August 1967: In this high profile pre-season friendly, FA Cup champions Tottenham faced European Cup winners Celtic as part of the QPR centenary celebrations at Hampden Park. The game ended in a 3-3 draw, with our goals scored by Jimmy Greaves (2) and Alan Gilzean.

6th August 2011: During this pre-season friendly against Athletic Bilbao, the atmosphere on the streets outside White Hart Lane was anything but friendly, as the London Riots started to brew. Whilst we were beating Athletic Bilbao 2-1, just down the road, as 300 people gathered outside Tottenham police station after marching from the Broadwater Farm estate. The protesters were demanding justice for the death of Mark Duggan, a local man who was shot dead by police two days earlier. Over the next few days, the rioting intensified, with several violent clashes and the destruction of many homes and businesses. The violence gained rapid media attention and spread throughout England, resulting in mass deployment of police and five deaths.

7th August 1899: 5,000 supporters gathered to watch Hotspur FC play their first football match at the-then-unnamed White Hart Lane. The first match was the third annual military tournament. The club had previously played at a pitch near Northumberland Park railway station that they shared with UCH rugby team, but with the ground becoming increasingly overcrowded, in 1899 the club moved a larger piece of land to the east of Tottenham High Road, behind the White Hart pub.

8th August 2015: Dele Alli made his Spurs debut in a Premier League defeat at Old Trafford when he came off the bench for the last 13 minutes. Dele made an impressive start to his Premier League career, scoring five goals in his first 18 league matches. In his first two seasons at the club, he was voted the PFA Young Player of the Year and was named in the PFA Team of the Year. In the 2019-20 season, new manager Jose Mourinho moved Dele back to his former position as an attacking player after playing as a midfielder the previous two seasons, a move that allowed him to score three goals in his first three games under Mourinho.

9th August 1969: In our earliest start to a campaign, we faced Leeds United in the old First Division. The FA decided to start the season early as they wanted to give the England team as much time as possible to prepare for the upcoming World Cup in Mexico. Spurs lost this match 3-1, our only goal being scored by Jimmy Greaves. The match marked the first League match back in almost a year for Martin Chivers following a serious knee injury in a home match against Nottingham Forest the previous September.

10th August 2019: Tanguy Ndombele scored on his Premier League debut for Spurs, helping us come from behind to beat Aston Villa 3-1. It was a game of two halves; newly-promoted Aston Villa surprised with their dominant performance in the first half but they sat back after the break as Spurs scored three times in the final 17 minutes to come back for the win. Harry Kane scored two, his first goals at the new Tottenham Hotspur Stadium.

11th August 2007: Younes Kaboul and Darren Bent made their Spurs debuts at newly-promoted Sunderland. Bent had recently transferred to Spurs for a club-record fee of £16.5 million. A 94th-minute goal from Sunderland sent us home with a 1-0 loss.

12th August 1967: Following an immense kick out of his hands, goalkeeper Pat Jennings famously scored his only Spurs goal in this Charity Shield against Manchester United at Old Trafford. In his 13 years at the club, Jennings made 591 appearances for Spurs, including 472 in League games. He won the FA Cup in 1967, the League Cup in 1971 and 1973, and the UEFA Cup in 1972.

13th August 2011: Our opening game of the season against Everton was cancelled due to safety concerns due to damage to the area around White Hart Lane following the London Riots. The rioting had initially started as a peaceful march, with protesters demanding justice for the death of Mark Duggan, a local man who was shot dead by police on 4th August. Over the next few days, the rioting intensified, with several violent clashes, arson and looting, that destroyed many homes and businesses and led to the death of five people.

14th August 2004: In a match against Liverpool, defender Noureddine Naybet became our oldest outfield debutant at 34 years 186 days. He was one of five debutants in the Spurs line-up that day. Naybet showed his experience with two crucial tackles. Jermain Defoe scored our equaliser in a 1-1 draw.

15th August 2013: Spurs announced that AIA Group Limited, the largest pan-Asian insurance company, was to become their Cup Shirt sponsor. The AIA Cup Shirt made its debut a week later in the first match of the Europa League against Dinamo Tbilisi. Spurs shirts have been sponsored since 1983 when they were first sponsored by Holsten Brewery.

16th August 2014: Eric Dier made his Spurs debut in the first match of the season away to West Ham. Spurs right-back Kyle Naughton received a red card when a handball prevented a scoring opportunity for West Ham. With the side down to 10 men, Dier moved to right-back from centre-back and marked his debut with a stoppage-time goal that gave Tottenham a 1-0 win.

17th August 2019: Hugo Lloris made his 300th appearance for the club in a League match against Manchester City. A dramatic stoppage-time winner from City made for an extraordinary finale that left the scoreboard at 3-2. The two sides returned to their dressing rooms and City supporters happily began their celebrations, but following mumblings of confusion, the late goal was overruled by VAR. The decision was based on a new rule, introduced only this season, stating that any goal resulting from handball, accidental or otherwise, must be ruled out. All of a sudden, the scoreboard changed back to 2-2 draw, and a little cheer rose up from the away crowd.

18th August 2013: Roberto Soldado scored a penalty on his Spurs debut to see us win 1-0 at Crystal Palace, inflicting Palace's first defeat in a top-flight match since 2005. Soldado was signed by Tottenham earlier that month in a record £26 million transfer deal with Valencia, a fee that far surpassed the club's previous record of £17 million paid for Paulinho earlier in the summer.

19th August 2009: In our first away game of the season, Jermain Defoe scored a hat-trick in our 5-1 win at Hull. Wilson Palacios and Robbie Keane also score. Defoe opened the scoring after 10 minutes, after collecting Tom Huddlestone's pass, before making a neat turn and shot that he powered into the far corner. Wilson Palacios then dashed onto Keane's pass four minutes later, to smash in his first and only goal for Spurs. Hull scored one, but Defoe fired home and restored our two-goal cushion just before half-time. In the second half, Robbie Keane scored the fourth with a header and Defoe then slammed in to complete his hat-trick in the final minute, with Spurs going to the top of the Premier League table.

20th August 1994: German World Cup star Jurgen Klinsmann made his Spurs debut in a match against Sheffield Wednesday. Initially, fans and media were sceptical of Klinsmann, partly because he played in the West Germany team that eliminated England from the 1990 World Cup and partly because of his reputation as a diver. In this debut match, he scored a header and celebrated with a self-deprecating dive, which immediately won over fans. In his first season at the club,

Klinsmann scored 21 goals for Spurs and won the 1995 Football Writers' Association Footballer of the Year award.

21st August 2010: Gareth Bale scored both goals in our 2-1 win at Stoke City, our first League win of the season. Bale's second goal was a stunning towering volley into the top right corner of the net, which was later awarded the BBC Goal of the Month. The brilliant goal even earnt a murmur of stifled approval from the Stoke supporters.

22nd August 2013: In the first leg of a Europa League match, we beat Dinamo Tbilisi 5-0 in Georgia. Andros Townsend put Tottenham ahead after an impressive 50-yard run that cut straight through the Dinamo defence. Roberto Soldado bagged a brace, Paulinho scored his first goal for Spurs, and Danny Rose scored the fifth to complete the 5-0 victory. The players wore the new AIA Cup Shirt for the first time, sponsored by AIA Group Limited, the largest insurance company in the world.

23rd August 2009: In our third successive win of the new season, we beat West Ham 2-1 away in a scrappy affair. West Ham took the lead but Jermain Defoe levelled just minutes later. Aaron Lennon then slammed in a late goal for the win. Three successive wins in the opening three games of the season was Tottenham's most successful start to a season for 49 years, since winning the "Double" in 1961.

24th August 1994: For the first time, all Spurs fans had a seat as White Hart Lane staged its first game as an all-seater stadium. However, only 24,533 spectators were actually able to watch due to ongoing refurbishments. Jurgen Klinsmann scored twice in his home debut, to see us beat Everton 2-1.

25th August 2011: In the second leg of a UEFA Europa League qualification match against Hearts, an 18-year-old Harry Kane made his Spurs debut. After comfortably winning the first leg 5-0, manager Harry Redknapp fielded six academy graduates in this second leg. Kane was awarded a penalty but he failed to convert it and the match ended in a goalless draw.

26th August 2009: An impressive 5-1 League Cup victory over Doncaster Rovers saw us cruise into the 3rd round of the Carling Cup. Tom Huddlestone scored the opener before Jamie O'Hara smashed in the second just minutes later. Peter Crouch scored his first goal for Spurs when he flicked in Bentley's corner, before Bentley scored his own for a fourth. Doncaster managed a consolation goal from a penalty but Roman Pavlyuchenko struck back, to leave Spurs with a brilliant 5-1 win.

27th August 1988: The opening match of the season was called off just six hours before kick-off due to overrunning building works at the stadium. The East Stand was being redeveloped throughout the summer but chairman Irving Scholar had been assured that the work would be completed before the start of the season. And even the night before our opening match against Coventry the club was still hoping the match could go ahead. But just six hours before kick-off, with debris still to be cleared, the authorities refused to issue the necessary safety certificate to allow the game to go ahead. It was a huge disappointment to the fans who had been eagerly awaiting the debut of new player Paul Gascoigne.

28th August 2015: In a transfer deal worth £22 million, Son Heung-min became the most expensive Asian player in football history when Tottenham signed him from Bayer Leverkusen. The previous record had been set in 2001 by Japanese player Hidetoshi Nakata, who transferred from Roma to Parma.

29th August 2013: Having beaten Dinamo Tbilisi 5-0 the previous week, a 3-0 win in the second leg saw Spurs breeze into the group stages of the Europa League. Jermain Defoe opened the scoring with two goals just before the interval. In the second half, Lewis Holtby bagged his first Spurs goal with a superb 25-yard strike off the bar and paid tribute to his German compatriot Jurgen Klinsmann with a celebration dive. Defoe's two goals moved him up to sixth place in the club's all-time goalscorers, where he still remains, with his 143 goals in 363 appearances.

30th August 1975: A 17-year-old Glenn Hoddle made his Spurs debut when he came on as a substitute for Cyril Knowles in a 2-2 draw with Norwich City. Hoddle went on to make 490 appearances for the club between 1975 and 1987 and scored 110 goals. Only four players have made more appearances for Spurs than Hoddle: Steve Perryman, Pat Jennings, Gary Mabbutt and Cyril Knowles.

31st August 2010: Two hours before the transfer window closed, the club made an offer of £8 million to Real Madrid for Dutch international Rafael Van der Vaart. With 83 international caps and 16 goals for the Netherlands, Van der Vaart was truly a world-class player, and his signing attracted significant media attention. The offer was a real signal of intent for Spurs and a demonstration of Harry Redknapp's vision for the direction of the club.

September

1st September 1908: Two months after being elected into the Second Division, Spurs played their first match in the English Football League, a home game against Wolves that we won 3-0. Vivian Woodward scored our first Football League goal after six minutes and added a second after the break. Tom Morris completed the scoring with a long-range strike.

2nd September 1967: A thumping 5-1 away defeat at Burnley brought an end to our record run of 28 League and Cup matches without defeat. The sequence had included 20 wins and 8 draws in 20 League and eight FA Cup matches. Jimmy Greaves scored our only goal in this 5-1 hammering.

3rd September 1988: After the first match of the season was postponed due to unfinished renovation work to the East Stand, new signing Paul Gascoigne instead made his Spurs debut against his former club, Newcastle United. On his arrival at St James' Park, Gascoigne was heckled by an aggrieved Newcastle crowd, who pelted him with Mars Bars. By half time, Newcastle had raced into a two-goal lead but goals from Chris Waddle and Terry Fenwick brought us back for a 2-2 draw.

4th September 1899: 5,000 fans thronged to our new stadium for the official opening of White Hart Lane. As the club started to grow in support, the decision was made to move the ground from Northumberland Park to this new ground behind the White Hart pub owned by Charringtons brewery. The official opening was marked with a 4-1 friendly victory over First Division Notts County. At the time, Tottenham were not even in the Football League.

5th September 1882: Hotspur FC was founded by a group of schoolboys from Tottenham Grammar School and St John's Presbyterian School, who were all members of the Hotspur Cricket Club. The group was led by 13-year-old Bobby Buckle who later became the club's first captain. The name "Hotspur" comes from "Harry Hotspur", a 14th-century knight who gained his nickname from his fearless heroics in battle. His real name was Sir Henry Percy and the Percy Family, descendents of the 1st Earl of Northumberland, owned land in the Tottenham area. He was also a keen cock fighter.

6th September 1998: Manager Christian Gross was sacked by chairman Alan Sugar after just nine months at the club. As a completely unknown name arriving at a club already fighting a relegation battle, Gross was under pressure from the off. And he got off to the worst possible start with a 6-1 home defeat to Chelsea. Goss endured a tough time throughout his tenure and was relentlessly ridiculed by the British tabloids. His poor results, and even worse communication skills, led to constant media criticism and the players became unresponsive to his management. When Spurs lost two of their opening three matches of the new season, Alan Sugar finally lost patience and dismissed Goss, blaming the media for destroying his reputation.

7th September 1968: Spurs thrashed Burnley 7-0, with goals scored by Cliff Jones (2), Jimmy Robertson, Jimmy Greaves (2 +1 penalty) and Martin Chivers. The win was the start of a successful three month period that saw only one defeat in 18 League and Cup games.

8th September 2004: Three Spurs players, Ledley King, Paul Robinson and Jermain Defoe, were in the line-up as England beat Poland 2-1 in this 2006 World Cup qualification match. Defoe scored the first goal of the match, his first international goal. Spurs have provided an incredible total of 78 England International players, more than any club.

9th September 1899: In the first competitive match to be played at White Hart Lane, we beat Queens Park Rangers 1-0, thanks to a goal by Tom Smith. Before we joined the Football League in 1908, Spurs played in three Leagues: the Southern League, the Western League and the London League as well as the various Cup competitions.

10th September 2016: In a comfortable 4-0 away win at Stoke, Son Heung-min proved his £22 million worth when he steered in a first-half opener before doubling our lead with another angled finish. Dele Alli added the third before Kane ended a nine-match goal drought when he fired Son's cross into an empty net from 3 yards, which pleased the Spurs fans enormously. The goal was Kane's 50th Premier League goal, the fourth Spurs player to reach the milestone, after Teddy Sheringham, Jermain Defoe and Robbie Keane. He achieved the feat in just 90 matches, faster than any other Spurs player in history and the 11th fastest of all football players.

11th September 1909: The old West Stand was officially opened for our first home game in the First Division against Manchester United. Robert Steel scored both our goals in a 2-2 draw. When Spurs were elected into the Football League the previous year, plans were drawn up by football ground architect Archibald Leitch to build a new stand. At a cost of £50,000, the West Stand became the largest stand at a British football ground, with 5,300 seats and a paddock for over 6,000 standing supporters. The roof covered the whole stand and featured a mock-Tudor gable, to which a copper cockerel and ball was added later in the season. The cockerel emblem has been synonymous with the club throughout its history and reflects Harry Hotspur's passion for cockfighting. Leitch built four stands for Spurs between 1909 and 1934.

12th September 1959: In one of our best ever performances at Old Trafford, Spurs triumphed 5-1 in a First Division match over Manchester United. Spurs took the lead with three first-half goals in ten minutes from Dave Dunmore, Bobby Smith and Tommy Harmer, but United pulled one back just before half-time. A facial injury meant Bobby Smith was unable to start the second half but we still managed to hold United off with just 10 men. Smith then came back on to score minutes from time before Dave Mackay scored his first goal for Spurs a minute later. Mackay went on to make 268 league appearances for Tottenham and was later chosen by the great Bill Nicholson as his best-ever signing.

13th September 1974: Terry Neill took over as manager following the departure of Bill Nicholson. As a former Arsenal player with no obvious links to Spurs, Neill was an unexpected, and not overly welcome, choice. He managed Spurs for two seasons, but struggled throughout, narrowly avoiding relegation in his first season and finishing mid-table in his second. It was no surprise then that the tenure came to an abrupt end after less than two years. What was perhaps more of a shock, given his poor results at Tottenham, was that Arsenal quickly snatched up Neill as their next manager.

14th September 2016: A record crowd of 85,011 watched us play AS Monaco in a Champions League Group E match at Wembley. It was the highest ever home attendance for an English club, but despite the atmosphere and expectation, Spurs failed to rise to the occasion and paid the price for their first-half sloppiness, as Monaco scored two goals and held on to win. Less than two months later, Spurs beat their own home-attendance record, when an even bigger crowd turned out for their match on 2nd November.

15th September 1951: Arthur Rowe's successful 'push and run' side set a club record for our best ever away win in the Football League, with a 6-1 victory over Stoke City. Spurs were the defending First Division champions, whilst Stoke was struggling at the bottom of the table, having conceded more goals than any other team. Tottenham showed their dominance, with first-half goals from Sid McClellan, Les Bennett and Alf Ramsey shooting us. After the break, Sonny Walters scored a spectacular fourth and Les Medley added two more before Stoke managed a consolation goal. The scoreline set a club record for our best ever away win in the Football League and remains our highest victory at Stoke City.

16th September 1916: In our first 'home' game at Highbury, we lost 2-3 to Luton Town in the London Combination. During the War, White Hart Lane was requisitioned by the War Office, and both Clapton Orient and Arsenal offered Tottenham the use of their grounds. For the next three seasons, Spurs alternated their games between the two grounds, playing 32 home games at Highbury.

17th September 2005: In a Premiership match at Aston Villa, Spurs fielded an entire team of international players for the first time. The team comprised England internationals Paul Robinson, Anthony Gardner, Ledley King, Jermaine Jenas, Robbie Keane, Michael Carrick and Jermain Defoe; Canadian international Paul Stalteri; Korean international Lee Young-pyo; Finnish international Teemu Tainio; Irish international Andy Reid; Moroccan international Noureddine Naybet and Polish international Grzegorz Rasiak. Robbie Keane came off the bench to earn Spurs a 1-1 draw.

18th September 2011: In an eventful game that saw seven yellow cards, Spurs took advantage of nine-man Liverpool, crushing them 4-0 at White Hart Lane. Croatian Luka Modric opened the scoring when he curled home a brilliant 25 yard shot on seven minutes, and Jermaine Defoe scored the second on 65 minutes. Emmanuel Adebayor marked his home debut for Spurs with two further goals to seal the 4-0 victory. The game ended with Harry Redknapp's players running continuous taunting passes around the helpless Liverpool, who had been reduced to just nine men.

19th September 1998: Dutch goalkeeper Hans Segers became our oldest debutant aged 36 years and 324 days. Segers was not the top choice of goalkeeper for the league game at Southampton, but both Espen Baardsen and Ian Walker had been taken ill. Segers put in a solid performance, only letting in one goal for a 1-1 draw. Then, in the last minute, Segers became the hero when Spurs defender Ramon Vaga mis-headed the ball towards the goal. Southampton leapt on the opportunity, making a powerful shot at point-blank range, but Segers made a heroic save.

20th September 1961: Spurs came back from a 2-4 deficit in the first leg to beat Polish club Gornik Zabrze 10-5 on aggregate. It was a preliminary round of the first European Champion Clubs' Cup and our first competitive European match. Spurs opened with a goal from Danny Blanchflower after nine minutes, before Cliff Jones struck in an impressive first-half hat-trick. Bobby Smith then headed in the fifth just before the break. In the second half, Smith scored again, and Terry Dyson and John White added another two, to see Tottenham win 8-1.

21st September 2003: Glenn Hoddle was sacked as manager after just two years in charge. Hoddle had a promising first season, being voted Premier League Manager of the Month for October 2001 and leading the team to the League Cup Final in 2002. At the start of the following season, Hoddle was again named Premier League Manager of the Month for August 2002 after we ended the month top of the League. But Spurs only managed to finish 10th in the table that season and the pressure began to build for Hoddle. After a poor start to his third season, in which the team picked up just four points from their opening six league games, Hoddle was sacked. David Pleat stepped in as caretaker manager.

22nd September 1934: The East Stand was officially opened for this home match against Aston Villa. The stand had been designed by football ground architect Archibald Leitch who built four stands for Spurs between 1909 and 1934. At a cost of £60,000, the new stand could accommodate 5,100 seated spectators and a further 18,700 in the terrace, increasing the ground capacity to nearly 80,000. Despite the much-increased capacity, only 42,088 people attended this match against Villa, fewer than the number who attended the fixture the previous season.

23rd September 2009: Peter Crouch scored his first hat-trick for Spurs in a 5-1 win over Preston North End, as we breezed into the fourth round of the Carling Cup. An unmarked Crouch volleyed Tottenham into the lead after 14 minutes and Jermain Defoe made it 2-0 with a header before half-time. Crouch slotted the ball into an empty net on 77 minutes, before Preston tapped home. Three minutes from time, Robbie Keane got the fourth, and Crouch completed his hat-trick with an audacious backheel just before the whistle. The scoreline was somewhat flattering for Spurs, but Harry Redknapp's team deserved the win.

24rth September 1983: In one of Spurs' greatest ever moments, Hoddle scored an incredible goal that brought Spurs back into the game from a goal down. After picking up the ball that was moving away from the goal, Hoddle quickly manoeuvred the ball around the hovering defender and coolly chipped the ball over the keeper into the corner of the net. Steve Archibald then came off the bench and nabbed a second goal, before Chris Hughton got the third. Watford managed a late goal but the game finished 3-2 to Spurs.

25th September 1968: In the third round of the League Cup, we faced Fourth Division Exeter City at White Hart Lane. Exeter City were very much the underdogs, but their fans were thrilled to be playing the prestigious Tottenham for the first time. Exeter opened the scoring but the goal of the match came in a moment of brilliance from Jimmy Greaves, who picked up the ball from Alan Gilzean and followed his left foot down-field, slaloming through the Exeter defence to score the equaliser. Unfortunately, keeper Pat Jennings then fumbled a shot from David Pleat and Exeter went back in front. Greaves scored his second and Venables scored another to put Spurs 3-2 ahead at half-time. After the break, Jimmy Pearce scored twice, his first goals for Spurs. Exeter battled on and scored again, but Jimmy Greaves was too good and scored his third in the final minute to complete his hat-trick and leave Spurs with a 6-3 win. Spurs went on to reach the semi-final, only to lose to Arsenal.

26th September 2015: Spurs thrashed Manchester City 4-1 and sealed a third successive Premier League win. City took the lead before Eric Dier equalised with a 25-yard shot on the half-time mark. Toby Alderweireld's header from an Erik Lamela free-kick put Spurs in front. Harry Kane side-footed in his first club goal of the season to make it 3-1 on 61 minutes after Christian Eriksen's free-kick bounced back off the crossbar. Erik Lamela slid home the fourth, to see Spurs brilliantly come from behind to win 4-1. It was the first time since 1962 that Tottenham had scored four goals in a League game against Manchester City.

27th September 1969: A 17-year-old Steve Perryman made his Spurs debut after joining as an apprentice. The 1-0 defeat to Sunderland may not have been anything to get fans excited, but the arrival of Perryman was the start of a special period for the club. Perryman went on to become one of Spurs' greatest ever players, making a record 800 appearances, including 656 League games and more than 550 games as captain. He won more trophies than any other Spurs player, including the UEFA Cup in 1972 and 1984, the FA Cup in 1981 and 1982, and the League Cup in 1971 and 1973. Playing between 1969 and 1986, Perryman was the club's longest serving player.

28th September 1983: Spurs beat Drogheda United 8-0 in a UEFA Cup first round match at White Hart Lane, adding to our six goals from the first leg. The goals in this match were scored by Graham Roberts (2), Steve Archibald, Alan Brazil (2), Mark Falco (2) and Chris Hughton. After winning the first round of the UEFA Cup 14–0 on aggregate, we progressed to the second round against Feyenoord. We continued to progress well through the rounds, making it all the way to the UEFA Cup Final on 23rd May 1984, where we played Anderlecht in perhaps the greatest night White Hart Lane has ever witnessed...

29th September 2012: In a match of extraordinary drama, Andre Villas-Boas' team ended a 23 year run of losses to finally beat Manchester United 2-3 at Old Trafford. Jan Vertonghen opened the scoring in the first two minutes and Gareth Bale doubled the lead, as Spurs played magnificently to take control of the first half. But United hit back in an explosive start to the second half that saw three goals scored in just 139 seconds; United scored in the 51st minute, only for Spurs to go straight up to the other end of the pitch and restore their two-goal cushion with a goal from Clint Dempsey, and the crowd barely had time to sit down before United struck again. The home side went on to dominate the remainder of the match, but they were unable to find an equaliser, as the match ended with a 3-2 victory to Spurs. The result delighted Spurs fans who had not seen a win at Old

Trafford since Gary Lineker scored the winner for Terry Venables' side in 1989.

30th September 1882: Only 25 days after the club was founded, Hotspur FC played our first ever recorded match. We lost 2-0 against a local team called the Radicals. The only other match that season was a game against Latymer when we again lost 8-1. The scorer was not recorded.

October

1st October 2019: In one of the darkest moments in the club's history, Bayern Munich inflicted a 7-2 thrashing in the Champions League, our heaviest home defeat by an English team in a European competition. Son Heung-min gave Spurs the lead in the 12th minute but Bayern struck back with two goals to take a 2-1 lead by the interval. After the break, former Arsenal player, Serge Gnabry, came back to haunt Spur when he scored two goals in two minutes. Harry Kane pulled one back with a penalty, but Bayern Munich scored another three, including two from Gnabry. It was the first time we had conceded seven goals in a competitive match since 1996, when we lost 7-1 to Newcastle United. It was Mauricio Pochettino's worst defeat as a manager and signalled the beginning of the end of his Spurs career.

2nd October 1983: Our 2-1 home win against Nottingham Forest was the first Football League game to be shown live in full on British television. It was a First Division match at White Hart Lane, with goals scored by Steve Archibald and Gary Stevens. In 1983, ITV had obtained a two-year contract from the Football League to show live matches for £5.2m. This was the first live League match to be shown since 1960.

3rd October 1987: Our 2-0 victory over Sheffield Wednesday was the last in our longest ever series of 14 consecutive home League wins, a record that still stands. The goals were scored by Paul Allen and Nico Claesen. The run, which began following a win against Aston Villa on 24th January 1987, spread over two seasons, the first nine at the end of the 1986-87 season and another five at the start of 1987-88. It came to an end when we were defeated by Arsenal on 18th October 1987.

4th October 1919: After moving from Edmonton Ramblers, Jimmy Dimmock made his Spurs debut in this League Division Two match away at Lincoln City that ended in a 1-1 draw. Our goal was scored by Albert Goodman. Dimmock is the only player in the club's history to play 400 League games and became the first to score 100 League goals for Spurs. He scored the winning goal in the 1921 FA Cup Final, a match in which he became (and remains) the youngest Tottenham player to appear in an FA Cup Final, at just 20 years 139 days.

5th October 1998: George Graham took over as manager. Graham started well, guiding the club to our first trophy in eight years with a victory over Leicester City in the 1999 League Cup Final, gaining a place in the UEFA Cup. But in his two seasons at the club, Graham could not finish higher than tenth in the table. In March 2001, soon after the club had been purchased by ENIC, Graham was sacked for "giving out what was deemed by the club as being private information". Earlier that week, Graham expressed his disappointment to the media with his "limited budget" for new players.

6th October 1883: In the club's first ever recorded win, Hotspur FC thrashed Brownlow Rovers 9-0. It was also the first Spurs game to be reported by the local paper, The Tottenham and Edmonton Weekly Herald.

7th October 2012: In this Premier League match against Aston Villa, manager Villas-Boas decided to play new keeper Hugo Loris, in favour of Brad Friedel, ending Friedel's run of 310 consecutive Premier League appearances. Loris played well, as we beat Villa 2–0 at White Hart Lane, with our goals scored by Steven Caulker and Aaron Lennon. Brad Friedel still remains the record-holder for most consecutive Premier League appearances, with 310 games during spells at Blackburn Rovers, Aston Villa and Spurs. In another record, Friedel still holds the record for being Spurs' oldest first-team player, when he appeared in a game against Newcastle United in November 2013, aged 42 years and 176 days.

8th October 1932: Following a poor start to the season, we were languishing near the bottom of Division Two. Manager Percy Smith decided to make some changes to the team for this game, and we went on to win 6-2 at Preston, with goals from Davie Colquhoun, Taffy O'Callaghan, George Hunt, George Greenfield and Willie Evans(2). The win marked a turning point for Spurs, and began a streak of 12 undefeated games, including eight wins, which saw them climb up the table. We finished the season second in the table, gaining promotion to the First Division.

9th October 2001: In this League Cup 3rd round match, Glenn Hoddle played a full-strength Spurs side to ensure there was no Cup shock against Second Division Tranmere Rovers. Tranmere did have an early moment of excitement, but Spurs were soon displaying superiority, mainly through Teddy Sheringham, who opened the scoring with a controversial 20th-minute penalty. Darren Anderton scored another before half-time. Gus Poyet scored the third early in the second half, before Sergei Rebrov scored his first goal of the season in the 81st minute. But the drama was not over as, just three minutes from time, Sherwood was harshly sent off with a second yellow card after fairly arguing that he should not have been penalised for handball, as the ball was fired under his arm from short range. Despite the red card, Spurs won a much-deserved 4-0 victory to see them progress to the 4th round of the League Cup.

10th October 1959: Film star and pin-up girl Jayne Mansfield was the main attraction in this highly anticipated First Division game against Wolves at White Hart Lane. Spurs were at the top of the League and unbeaten in our opening 11 fixtures, while reigning champions Wolves were in second place divided only by goal average. Bobby Smith scored four of our goals, including a spectacular overhead kick, but not even a stunning 5-1 victory was enough to steal the limelight from Jayne Mansfield in the box. In a slightly outdated description, one journalist reported: "...to add to the excitement and entertainment actress Jayne Mansfield, who occupied a place in the stand, not to be outdone in the way of figures, took off her outer wrappings to display her sensational figure to the crowd at half-time." And in another scene perhaps representative of the 1950s, Cliff Jones later recalled going "into the directors' room afterwards and Fred Bearman, who was chairman at the time, ended up with her sitting on his knee".

11th October 1958: Bill Nicholson took charge for the first time following Jimmy Anderson's retirement earlier that day. Despite leading Spurs to the FA Cup semi-final in 1956, a poor League performance and a public falling out with captain Danny Blanchflower, ultimately led to Anderson's early retirement. Nicholson took over a club languishing in the bottom half of the First Division but, in his first game in charge, Tottenham beat Everton 10-4 at White Hart Lane, setting a new club record. The record has only once been surpassed when we beat Crewe Alexandra 13-2 in the 1960 FA Cup.

12th October 1996: In a home game against Aston Villa, Justin Edinburgh became our 1,000th substitute to come off the bench in a League match. Manager Gerry Francis put out a strong side that included five internationals: Teddy Sheringham, Ian Walker and Sol Campbell (all England), Colin Calderwood (Scotland) and Alan Nielsen (Denmark). Alan Nielsen scored his first goal for Spurs to win the game 1-0, our first victory over Villa in 12 games. This match became infamous when Aston Villa keeper, Mark Bosnich, aimed a Nazi salute at Tottenham fans. Bosnich was found guilty of misconduct and fined £1,000 and censured by the FA.

13th October 1894: In our first ever FA Cup match, and in front of a crowd of 2,000 people, we defeated Watford-based West Herts 3-2 in a home game at Northumberland Park. Spurs led 2-0 at half-time with goals from Peter Hunter and Donald Goodall. However, in the second half West Herts came racing out of the blocks and scored within five minutes and then levelled shortly after, before Goodall scored the winner. We would meet Clapton in the next round. The home ground at Northumberland Park, between the railway tracks and the River Lea, had been Tottenham's home ground since they moved from their first ground at Tottenham Marshes in 1888.

14th October 1967: In our 2,000th Football League match, we beat Coventry City 3-2 in a First Division game at Highfield Road. Jimmy Greaves scored two and Cliff Jones scored the third.

15th October 1927: Frank Osborne scored our 500th point in the First Division in a 1-1 home draw against Blackburn Rovers at White Hart Lane.

16th October 1920: A record 76,000 League game crowd turned out to watch us play a First Division match against Chelsea at Stamford Bridge. We won 4-0 with goals from Wilson (2), Dimmock and Bliss. The scoreline remains the biggest victory at Stamford Bridge, being equalled only once on 30th September 1933.

17th October 1885: In our first ever competitive match, Hotspur FC faced St Albans in the London Association Cup. Four hundred spectators watched us beat St Albans 5-2 at our first home ground at Tottenham Marshes. The Spurs team included six of the club's founder members, with Harston, Mason (2) and Amos (2) scoring our goals. But the success did not last long, as we sustained a heavy 8-0 defeat in the next round to the Casuals, one of the biggest names in football's early history.

18th October 2016: A UEFA Champions League group stage match against Bayer Leverkusen ended in a goalless draw. Hugo Lloris made six excellent saves, including a spectacular one-handed stop in the 48th minute. Manager Mauricio Pochettino praised Lloris's performance as "brilliant".

19th October 2006: Hossam Ghaly and Dimitar Berbatov were on the mark for Tottenham as we beat Besiktas 2-0 in our opening UEFA Cup Group stage match in Istanbul. Just after the half-hour mark, Berbatov controlled Robinson's long clearance and passed to Ghaly who made a shot; it was initially saved by the Besiktas goalkeeper, but the ball then rebound off Ghaly's knee and looped into the net for a lucky first goal. Then in the second half, Berbatov slotted home a second with a fine solo goal. Under the management of Martin Jol, we continued to progress well in the 2006-07 UEFA Cup, but were knocked out in the quarter-finals by the eventual winners, Sevilla.

20th October 2010: In an eventful Champions League group stage away leg against Inter Milan, Bale scored his first Spurs hat-trick to help bring us back from a four-goal deficit. In an explosive start, Inter Milan scored in the second minute, before our goalkeeper, Heurelho Gomes, was sent off with a red card, leaving us down to 10 men and more than 80 minutes of the game left to play. With our goal wide open, Inter struck in another two, leaving us 3-0 down in the first 14 minutes. And by 35 minutes, we were 4-0 down. But after the break, Spurs valiantly battled back, with Bale smashing in after a surging run down the left. It remained 4-1 until the final two minutes, which were as sensational as Inter's opening 15 minutes, when Bale scored an almost identical second, before rapidly firing in a third in the dying moments of the match, to complete his stunning second-half hat-trick.

Despite narrowly losing the match, Bale's momentous efforts made this a match to remember. We faced Inter Milan again for the home leg just two weeks later on 2nd November in an equally exciting match.

21st October 1950: In this First Division match, we beat Stoke City 6-1 at the Lane. Les Bennett (2), Len Duquemin (2), Lesley Medley and Sonny Walters all scored. We went on to win the First Division, having won the Second Division the previous season. The early 1950s were an exciting time for Tottenham, led by manager Arthur Rowe, who pioneered the "push and run" style of play.

22nd October 1977: A 9-0 win over Bristol Rovers at White Hart Lane saw Spurs set a record for the biggest win of the Football League. This game is one of only six occasions the Spurs have scored nine goals in a League game. It was Spurs' first season out of the top division since 1950 and they were determined to return to regain a promotion. The season had started well with eight unbeaten games, but Tottenham came into this match on the back of a defeat at Charlton, and were desperate for a win. New striker Colin Lee made a perfect debut as he scored four of our nine goals. By the end of the first half, we were up 3-0, with two from Lee and another from Peter Taylor. After the break, Spurs upped their play further, with a third from Lee and a hat-trick from Ian Moores, to make it 7-0. Two minutes from time, Lee capped off a memorable debut when he tapped home his fourth. But the best was yet to come. With the fans already celebrating, Hoddle volleyed in a magnificent shot to seal Spurs' 9-0 victory. At the final whistle, hundreds of joyous spectators swarmed onto the pitch, with the police and stewards battling to hold them back. The win, which got top billing on Match of the Day, proved to be a hugely important win as, at the end of the season, Spurs were promoted on goal difference alone, with a goal difference of exactly nine goals.

23rd October 1999: In a Premiership game against Manchester United at White Hart Lane, Stephen Carr treated us to one of the greatest ever Spurs moments. United took the lead, but Steffen Iversen equalised after 36 minutes and United helped us out with an own goal three minutes later, putting us 2-1 ahead at half-time. In the second half, Manchester United threw all they could into attack, battling on in the driving rain. Beckham, incensed by several refereeing decisions, received his fifth yellow card of the season, earning himself a suspension. United did a bit of re-shuffle with their players, and taking advantage of the adjustments, Spurs full-back Stephen Carr picked up the ball in his own half and ran up the pitch before unleashing a cracking shot into the top corner from 25 yards out. The spectacular strike was his first home goal for Spurs and was subsequently voted the Goal of the Season. To add to the magic, the 3-1 victory was our first League win over United for nearly four years.

24th October 1962: In a 6-2 victory over Manchester United, we scored our 2,000th goal in the First Division. One goal from Jimmy Greaves and two from Terry Medwin, put Spurs 3-0 ahead by half-time. In the second half, Greaves scored his second and Cliff Jones got the fifth, before Greaves completed his hat-trick for the sixth. United battled back with two late goals, but it was not enough to catch the mighty Spurs.

25th October 2007: After reaching the quarter-finals of the UEFA Cup earlier in the year, the club had signed a number of expensive players, spending around £40 million. It was reported that then-manager Martin Jol was not consulted about the signings and had little control over the selection of new players. But having spent so much money, the Board were expecting a top-four finish. Having lost the opening two games of the season, Jol was under pressure, before the Board made the decision to sack him during Spurs' 2–1 defeat to Getafe CF in the UEFA Cup. News of the sacking spread throughout the group while the match was still playing, and even before Jol had been told. In fact, Jol first became aware of the decision when his nephew told him of the news that had been circulating.

26th October 2008: Harry Redknapp was appointed as manager, and his first match was against Bolton Wanderers. Redknapp's managerial style was focused more on motivating and energising players rather than on skill or tactics, but his arrival had an immediately galvanising effect on the club that had been struggling in the League. In his first match in charge, Redknapp's men beat Bolton Wanderers 2-0, when Roman Pavlyuchenko scored a first-half goal, before Darren Bent wrapped up the win with a penalty after he was fouled by the Bolton goalkeeper. The 2-0 victory was Tottenham's first League win of the season, and their first home win since March when they beat Redknapp's former club Portsmouth. Despite remaining bottom of the table, the gloom was beginning to lift, and the win marked the beginning of an entertaining four years at the club.

27th October 2009: Goals from Tom Huddlestone and Robbie Keane saw us knock Everton out of the Carling Cup and book our place in the quarter-finals. Everton had won on each of their previous three visits to the Lane but, on this occasion, history was not to be repeated. Huddlestone thumped the ball home just after the half hour mark to give Spurs the lead. Everton came close to levelling after half-time, but Heurelho Gomes put in a good save. Then on 57 minutes, Keane took a penalty. The strike was saved by the Everton keeper, but a bizarre goalmouth scramble ensued, and Keane took the chance to drive the ball into the roof of the net, to see us win 2-0.

28th October 1972: A stylish performance and four goals from Martin Peters gave us a comfortable 4-1 victory over Manchester United, our first win at Old Trafford in the past 10 games. Martin Peters signed for Tottenham in March 1970 from West Ham and as part of a record-breaking £200,000 deal. Peters captained the Spurs team to the League Cup win over Norwich City in 1973 and during his five years at the club, he made 260 appearances, scoring 66 goals. In the early 1970s, Peters formed a successful attacking trio with Martin Chivers and Alan Gilzean that worked together to help each other to create and score many goals for Spurs.

29th October 2016: We drew 1-1 against defending League Champions Leicester City at White Hart Lane. Overall, we were the much better team, as strong as ever in defence and creating multiple opportunities; Dele Alli and Jan Vertonghen both hit the crossbar. Vincent Janssen gave Spurs the lead in the 44th minute, scoring his first Premier League goal when he converted from the penalty spot after he had been fouled. But the Foxes equalised shortly after the break, taking advantage of one slip up from Victor Wanyama. It was hugely frustrating. Not only was this the first goal that we had conceded from open play this season, but it was also against our rivals who had pipped us to the title last season.

30th October 2013: After 19 years and seven failed attempts, Tottenham finally won a penalty shootout, to advance to the quarter-finals of the League Cup. The victory was against Hull City, a team who we had played just three days earlier in a Premier League match, also at White Hart Lane. We knew we could win, but Hull turned out to be a little more stubborn than they had been just a few days before. In this Cup match, Gylfi Sigurdsson's 25-yard strike put us 1-0 ahead at half-time, but Spurs keeper Brad Friedel fumbled into his own net, leaving it 1-1 at 90 minutes. The match went to extra time, and Hull took the lead, before a low shot from substitute Harry Kane sent the game to a penalty shoot-out. Both teams missed one penalty each in the first five kicks, but Brad Friedel made up from his previous error to crucially deny a Hull and give Spurs a 8-7 win on penalties.

31st October 1962: In the 1st round of the European Cup Winners' Cup, Spurs beat Glasgow Rangers 5-2 in the first leg. It was a hard-fought game that saw three of our goals set up by Jimmy Greaves corners. Just four minutes in, White headed in our first goal from a Jimmy Greaves corner. Rangers quickly equalised before White repeated his header from another Greaves corner. Les Allen made it 3-1, and with the Rangers defence under pressure, they conceded an own goal. However, they pulled one back to make it 4-2, before Mauric Norman scored our fifth from another Greaves corner ten minutes from time, to leave the final score 5-2. In this match, the Spurs players wore long-sleeved crew neck shirts for the first time, replacing the short sleeved shirts that had been worn since 1959.

November

1st November 1994: After only 18 months in charge, Ossie Ardiles was dismissed as manager. Unfortunately, Ardiles was nowhere near as successful as a manager as he had been as a player. Despite the expensive purchase of Jürgen Klinsmann, Ilie Dumitrescu and Gheorghe Popescu earlier in the year, Tottenham were languishing in the bottom half of the Premier League, and Ardiles was sacked.

2nd November 2010: Following a thrilling Champions League away leg in Milan on 20th October, Inter Milan made the return for a memorable night at White Hart Lane. Rafael van der Vaart opened the scoring in the 18th minute, continuing his strong record of scoring in every home game since joining the club. Gareth Bale then brilliantly set up our second goal for Peter Crouch to score. The crowd was going wild for Bale, whose unstoppable power and superb pace left the defending European Champions helpless. Bale was beyond containment and Tottenham continued to overwhelm the opposition in devastating style. Inter pulled one back in the 80th minute but then, a minute from time, Bale burst down the left and rolled the ball into the middle to be met by substitute Roman Pavlyuchenko who struck in our third. The outstanding 3-1 win against the Champions League holders was a giant stride towards the last 16 of the Champions League.

3rd November 2013: In a goalless match at Everton, goalkeeper Hugo Lloris suffered a heavy knock to the head and lost consciousness after diving at the feet of an Everton striker during the second half. Lloris initially looked set to go off on a stretcher but, after a lengthy delay, he appeared to argue with the medical team to play on. After the match, manager André Villas-Boas said Lloris "showed great character and personality", but the decision to allow him to play on was heavily criticised by head injury charities, FIFA and the players' union, FIFPro, who deemed the club highly irresponsible. In response, Spurs said Lloris was cleared by the club's medical team.

4th November 1899: In this Southern League game, Hotspur FC won an impressive 7-0 victory over Thames Ironworks, who would later become West Ham. Tom Pratt scored three for the club's first ever recorded hat-trick. Before joining the Football League in 1908, Spurs played in three Leagues, the Southern League, the Western League and the London League as well as the various Cup competitions.

5th November 2006: Spurs finally beat Chelsea, ending a humiliating 16-year run of League defeats, that had inspired Chelsea fans to nickname our ground 'Three Points Lane'. In this match, Chelsea took an early lead, but manager Martin Jol responded by switching to a 4-5-1 formation with Lennon moving to the right wing and Keane pulling back to the left flank. It proved an excellent response, and goals from Michael Dawson and Aaron Lennon saw Tottenham come back back from a goal down to finally lift the hex that Chelsea had held over the club since 1990.

6th November 2008: Less than two weeks after Harry Redknapp had taken over as manager, Spurs looked rejuvenated and put on their best performance of the season, to thrash Dinamo Zagreb 4-0 at White Hart Lane in the UEFA Cup group stages. Bent smashed home in the 29th minute before calmly slotting in Huddlestone's pass three minutes later. Huddlestone then fired in his own long-range volley in the 58th minute, before Bent completed his hat-trick with 20 minutes to go. Young debutant John Bostock then came off the bench in the 80th minute, becoming, at 16 years 295 days old, Spurs' youngest ever player in a competitive game.

7th November 2013: Tottenham won 2-1 against Sheriff Tiraspoln of Moldova to progress to the knockout stages of the Europa League. Erik Lamela opened the scoring with a calm strike on 60 minutes, his first goal for the club. Lamella then continued his excellent work with a dazzling run then ended in him being fouled in the penalty area. Jermain Defore converted the penalty, to score his 23rd European goal for Spurs, overtaking Martin Chivers's 39-year record as the club's European top scorer. Sheriff Tiraspoln scored a late goal but Spurs held on to progress in the Europa League.

8th November 2012: Jermain Defoe scored a brilliant hat-trick in a 3-1 win against Slovenian club NK Maribor in this Europa League group stage match. Defoe's hat-trick took him to 126 goals for Tottenham, moving him above Teddy Sheringham to eighth place on the club's all-time list. When he was substituted off on 82 minutes, Defoe received a standing ovation.

9th November 2008: Revitalised under new manager Harry Redknapp, Spurs continued an unbeaten run, as we won our first away win of the season, beating Manchester City 2-1. Man City scored first before a second bookable offence took them down to just 10 men following. Bent took advantage and slotted home the equaliser just three minutes later. Spurs continued the stronger team and Bent got his second after the break to make the score 2-1. Spurs' Benoit Assou-Ekotto was dismissed a minute from time but the game was already over. This match was Ledley King's 250th appearance for Tottenham.

10th November 2013: American goalkeeper Brad Friedel made his final appearance for Spurs in a home game against Newcastle United. At 42 years 176 days old, he became (and still remains) our oldest first-team player. Sadly, this was not Friedel's best game as we lost 1-0, and fans questioned whether Lloris, who was off following a head injury the previous week, might have done better. André Villas-Boas argued that Friedel was not to blame for the defeat, although Alan Pardew, the Newcastle manager, said that his team had "capitalised on what we thought was a little weakness on their part".

11th November 1964: The John White Memorial match was held in memory of Spurs legend and Scottish international John White, who tragically died aged 27 when struck with lightning while playing golf. The match was held at White Hart Lane, where we played a Scotland XI, losing 2-6. Over 29,000 spectators attended the game which had been postponed from the previous night because of fog. John's brother, Tommy, appeared as a guest player for Spurs, scoring one of the goals with the other coming from Tony Marchi. Two of the Scotland XI's goals were scored by Alan Gilzean who Spurs signed from Dundee just a few weeks later. John White had been a key member of the 'Double' team, and was highly regarded for his excellent passes, tight ball control and swift runs. Spurs fans nicknamed him "The Ghost" as he would often arrive unexpectedly in the penalty area. With White, Tottenham never finished worse than 4th in the First Division and of the 15 matches White missed, Tottenham only won one.

12th November 2008: Reigning champions Tottenham cruised into the quarter-finals of the Carling Cup with a thrilling 4-2 victory over Liverpool. Spurs raced into a 3-0 lead with a devastating six-minute spell that saw three goals from Roman Pavlyuchenko and Fraizer Campbell (2). Liverpool pulled one back after the break, but Tottenham quickly snuffed out any threat of a Liverpool comeback when Pavlyuchenko netted his second goal of the match. It was an excellent performance from Spurs who, rejuvenated under new manager Harry Redknapp, dominated throughout.

13th November 2004: A 5-4 defeat to Arsenal at White Hart Lane set a record for the most individual goal scorers in a Premiership game and still stands as the highest scoring North London Derby. It was Martin Jol's first Premiership match since taking over as head coach from Jacques Santini. Towards the end of an uneventful first half, the game burst into life as Noureddine Naybet volleyed in, before Arsenal levelled. In the second half, Arsenal stuck in a penalty at 53 minutes, then scored again on the hour over a diving Paul Robinson to make it 3-1. Jermain Defoe then lit up the stadium after beating three Arsenal players to strike only a minute later (3-2). After a brief moment of hope for Spurs fans, Arsenal restored their two-goal lead, but Spurs legend Ledley King got Spurs' third with a header. Arsenal scored their fifth, but Spurs were not giving up, as Frédéric Kanouté brought the score to 5-4 just two minutes from time.

14th November 2019: Two Spurs players shon in this England international match at Wembley, where a 7-0 victory over Montenegro secured England's qualification place for Euro 2020. Harry Kane's first-half hat-trick brought his tally of international goals up to 31, and during the course of the game, Kane overtook Vivian Woodward, Frank Lampard, Tom Finney, Alan Shearer and Nat Lofthouse, to move into sixth in the list of England's all-time goal-scorers. His goals also brought his total number of England goals as captain to 24, to see him move ahead of Spurs legend Vivian Woodward as the highest-scoring England captain. But Harry Kane wasn't the only Spur to impress in this match. Harry Winks also put in an excellent performance, pressing the team forward up the pitch and denying the opposition any time on the ball. Winks was doing perfectly what Spurs used to do so well.

15th November 1994: Gerry Francis was appointed as manager following the sacking of Ossie Ardiles, making him the third Spurs manager in two years. During his playing career, Francis had played for

QPR and captained England but he grew up as a Spurs fan, supporting the club during the glory, glory days of the early 1960s. In his first season in charge, Francis brought the team up away from the chaos of Ossie Ardiles' reign and took us to 7th place in the Premier League, the highest London club that season. He also led us to the FA Cup semis. But we finished mid table in the next two seasons and, with Spurs battling in the relegation zone, Francis resigned in November 1997. During his time at Tottenham, Francis became resented by the fans over his handling of star player Darren "sick-note" Anderton. It has been argued that Francis was responsible for Anderton's recurring injuries, placing him in the team without sufficient time to recover.

16th November 1991: In this home game against Luton Town, Spurs were 1-0 down in the second half and looked likely to lose this game when the floodlights failed, plunging the pitch into semi darkness. The club's precarious financial state at the time was not lost on the crowd, who piped up with witty comments about putting a pound in the meter, getting the candles out, and not being able to afford the electricity bill. When the game resumed 15 minutes later, Spurs were a new team and fought back scoring four goals in the last quarter to win 4-1. Substitute Scott Houghton equalised, scoring his first goal for Spurs, before scoring a second. Gary Lineker also scored twice.

17th November 2001: This was Glenn Hoddle's first home North London Derby in charge, but the game was completely overshadowed by the return of Sol Campbell who had defected to Arsenal during the summer. Campbell's reception was predictably hostile, with Spurs fans holding up banners and white balloons reading "Judas". Both on and off the pitch, the atmosphere at the Lane was highly charged, and the game started with an early scrap between Martin Keown and Les Ferdinand, who were both booked for their hostilities. Amongst the chaos, it took until the 81st minute before a goal was scored by

Arsenal. Gus Poyet equalised with a volley to leave the final score at 1-1.

18th November 1950: In a highly anticipated game, the highest crowd of the season gathered at White Hart Lane to watch newly promoted and fourth-place Tottenham take on second-place Newcastle United. Goals from Les Bennett, Eddie Baily and Les Medley put us up 3-0 by half-time. In the second half, Spurs continued their excellent display, as Medley scored the fourth and Sonny Walters got the fifth before Medley completed his hat-trick. Alf Ramsey scored the final goal from the penalty spot to see us beat Newcastle United 7-0.

19th November 2019: Mauricio Pochettino was dismissed as manager after more than five years in charge. During his time at the club, Pochettino transformed Spurs' fortunes. Prior to his arrival, the club had managed only two top-four finishes in 22 Premier League seasons, but Pochettino achieved the feat on four out of his five seasons in charge. He also led the club to our first ever Champions League Final. However, domestic results had been on the decline, with just three wins in 12 games, and the club sitting 14th in the League. Chairman Daniel Levy cited these "extremely disappointing" domestic results for the dismissal, but many fans blamed the poor results on the club itself, suggesting they were the consequence of not signing any new players in the previous two transfer windows. Pochettino had warned the club what would happen without signings, but with the expense of the new stadium, the club believed it wasn't the time to invest in new players. Whatever your side, Pochettino will go down as one of the great Tottenham managers.

20th November 2019: Following the dismissal of Pochettino the day before, Jose Mourinho took over as manager. Pochettino was hugely popular with the Tottenham faithful and Mourinho's allegiance to Chelsea and his acrimonious departure from Manchester United means he has work to do to win over the fans. But we have reason to be hopeful. His down-to-earth character and strong history of success could win over even the most faithful Pochettino supporters. In chairman Daniel Levy's words, "In Jose we have one of the most successful managers in football". It is true. Of all the Premier League managers, Jose Mourinho is the quickest to reach both 50 and 100 wins. Mourinho has won 135 of 193 Premier League games as a manager, making his win percentage a huge 70%, better than any other manager in Premier League history. And, on taking over in 2019, Mourinho was only 10 wins away from reaching 200 Premier League victories, a feat only achieved by four managers: Sir Alex Ferguson, Arsene Wenger, Harry Redknapp and David Moyes. The future looks bright for Spurs.

21st November 2017: Spurs came from behind to beat Borussia Dortmund 2-1 away in a UEFA Cup group stage match, to finish top of a tough Group H. After falling a goal down, Harry Kane scored Tottenham's equaliser before Son Heung-min sealed the victory. The game followed a 3-1 win against Real Madrid. Kane later said that Tottenham proved the doubters wrong by finishing top of one of the toughest groups in the Champions League.

22nd November 2009: In our biggest ever Premier League win, a 9-1 home win over Wigan Athletic 9-1 set records for the highest number of goals scored in one half of Premier League football (9), and for the highest number of goals scored by one team in one half of Premier League football (8). Jermain Defoe scored five of the goals, equalling a Premier League record for most goals scored in a game by a single player.

23rd November 2019: In Mourinho's first game in charge, Son scored the first goal in an away match against West Ham. After a generally uneventful start to the match, Son got the first and Lucas Moura scored again just before the interval. Harry Kane extended Tottenham's lead with a trademark header four minutes into the second half to move into third place on the list of the club's all-time scorers on 175 goals. West Ham reduced the deficit with two late goals, but Spurs held on to win 3-2. This was the first Spurs away win since January, a point not lost on Mourinho, who said after the match, "Eleven months without music in the away dressing room. I am very happy for them."

24th November 2018: We inflicted Chelsea's first Premier League defeat of the season when we beat them 3-1 to leapfrog above them to third in the table. A flicked header from Dele Alli and a well-placed cross from Christian Eriksen gave us two goals in the first 16 minutes, before Harry Kane fired in the third from long range.

25th November 2000: Les Ferdinand scored all three goals in our 3-0 home win over Leicester City, our eighth successive unbeaten home League game of the season. Ferdinand scored twice in a five-minute spell in the first half, before completing his hat-trick six minutes from time. The win saw Tottenham climb to seventh in the League, easing the pressure on manager George Graham.

26th November 2019: Jose Mourinho made a dramatic entrance in his first home game in charge as Tottenham came back from two goals down to beat Olympiakos 4-2 and secure our place in the last 16 of the UEFA Champions League. Mourinho made a low-key entrance for his first game, but after the whistle blew, there was nothing low-key about the game. But the game was far less comfortable than that scoreline appears. Far from Mourinho's dream start, Spurs were dreadful in the first half, being run ragged by Olympiakos who were exposing so many of the flaws in the team that led to Pochettino's dismissal. We went behind after just six minutes, before conceding a second 13 minutes later. Mourinho acted by sending on Christian Eriksen, but it still took a horrendous error from Olympiakos to hand Dele Alli a goal in first-half stoppage time. But after the interval, Spurs emerged a different side. Harry Kane levelled cross five minutes after the break, and defender Serge Aurier took the lead with a powerful finish 17 minutes from time. Mourinho fist-pumped in delight and he was ecstatic again when Kane wrapped things up when he headed in Eriksen's free-kick.

27th November 2014: Scoring his first goal for Spurs, Benjamin Stambouli pounced on a loose ball to give Spurs a 1-0 victory over Partizan Belgrade, and secure Tottenham's position in the Europa League knockout stages. But the achievement was overshadowed by three first-half pitch intruders, who forced the referee to suspend the match. The players withdrew for 10 minutes before re-emerging to play what remained of the first half.

28th November 2010: In this thrilling roller-coaster of a Premier League game, Spurs came back from a goal down to beat Liverpool 2-1. Spurs went behind before the break and Jermain Defoe missed a penalty, but an own-goal from Liverpool brought us level. Aaron Lennon then struck an injury-time winner to earn Tottenham a dramatic last-minute win and move Harry Redknapp's side to within six points the League table leaders.

29th November 2015: Tottenham extended their unbeaten run to 13 League games in an uneventful goalless draw with Chelsea at White Hart Lane. It was a slow game with neither side able to break through the other's defence, but the Chelsea keeper had a bit of work to do in the first half, saving a few shots-on-target from Harry Kane, Son Heung-min and Mousa Dembele. In their previous ten Premier League visits to White Hart Lane, Chelsea had won only once.

30th November 2019: After a dramatic late comeback from Bournemouth, Spurs managed to hold on to win 3-2 at the new Tottenham Hotspur stadium. Two goals from Dele Alli and another from Moussa Sissoko saw Spurs take a strong 3 goal lead. But with the score still 3-0 in the final quarter, Bournemouth then mounted a dramatic fightback, scoring two late goals. Spurs did enough to hold them off, to win the game at 3-2 and move up to fifth in the table.

December

1st December 2013: In a match against Manchester United, Man U equalised twice, as they fought back twice to deny Tottenham a much-needed victory. After 20 minutes the game exploded into life when Paulinho won a free-kick, which Kyle Walker pelted under the United wall to put Spurs ahead. Man United, though the weaker side throughout the opening half, managed an equaliser following a mistake from a Phil Jones cross. In the second half, Sandro's ferocious 25-yard strike curled into the top corner to restore Spurs' lead, but, minutes later the visitors were level again converting a dubious penalty, to leave the score 2-2.

2nd December 1916: In a 'home' game at Highbury, Tottenham beat Arsenal 4-1. Jimmy Banks bagged a hat-trick. During the War, White Hart Lane was requisitioned by the War Office, and both Clapton Orient and Arsenal offered Tottenham the use of their grounds. For the next three seasons, Spurs alternated their games between the two grounds, playing 32 home games at Highbury.

3rd December 2011: Tottenham beat 10-man Bolton 3-0 at home to go second in the Premier League table. Gareth Bale got the ball rolling in the sixth minute, knocking in a corner from close range. He celebrated the goal by holding up his left boot with "R.I.P Gary Speed" stitched on it, a tribute to his former Wales International manager, Gary Speed. Speed had died less than a week earlier and had previously played for Bolton. The Bolton goalkeeper produced a string of excellent saves for his 10-man team but his heroics could not stop Aaron Lennon from doubling our lead in the 50th minute. Jermain Defoe then swept in the third on the hour. The game finished in a comfortable 3-0 victory, but Spurs could have won by far more, such was their dominance over Bolton. The win was our 11th Premier League match without defeat, equalling a previous club record.

4th December 2004: In Spurs' first away win in the league under new coach Martin Jol, Robbie Keane scored the only goal of this match against Blackburn Rovers. Spurs were better than the scoreline suggests, playing with more power and creativity, and firing more shots on target than Blackburn. Midway through the second half, Michael Brown set up the only goal of the match when he picked up the ball on the halfway line, shrugged off a tackle, before snaking through the static Rovers defence and picking out Keane, who coolly slotted the ball in past future Spurs keeper Brad Friedel. Once Robbie Keane had given us the lead, Spurs showed discipline in fortifying our defence to deny Blackburn any comeback.

5th December 1992: In a home game against Chelsea at White Hart Lane, Sol Campbell made his first-team debut when he came on as a substitute, to net a late consolation only goal in a 2–1 defeat. Following his debut, Campbell was not picked by manager Terry Venables again throughout the remainder of the season. Campbell went on to become a favourite at the Lane until his unforgivable betrayal in 2001.

6th December 2003: In a home game against Wolves, a comfortable 5-2 win sent Wolves down to the bottom of the table. Keane opened the scoring in the 29th minute when he struck in from six yards to give Spurs the lead. Freddie Kanoute headed in Darren Anderton's cross from Spurs' second after the break, before Robbie Keane completed his hat-trick. Substitute Stephane Dalmat added a late fifth in the 90th minute.

7th December 2019: In a Premier League game at the new Tottenham Hotspur Stadium, we inflicted an impressive 5-0 defeat over Burnley. Harry Kane scored a stunning long-range strike after just four minutes and, by 10 minutes, we were 2-0 up thanks to a second goal from Lucas Moura who tucked in from close range. Son Heung-min then made it 3-0 by half-time when he picked up the ball and sprinted 70 yards from one end of the pitch to the other, past seven stunned Burnley players, to coolly slot home. It was an outstanding individual goal that was later awarded the Premier League goal of the month. Jose Mourinho called Son "Sonaldo Nazario" in reference to the type of goal Ronaldo would have scored. In the second half, a powerful finish from Harry Kane, and a Moussa Sissoko strike, saw us cruise to a 5-0 victory. Tottenham had now won eight of their last nine home games against Burnley in all competitions, drawing the other.

8th December 2008: Harry Redknapp returned to his old stomping ground to see Tottenham beat West Ham United. Redknapp had spent seven years in charge of West Ham, and on his arrival at Upton Park for this match, he was met with resounding boos from a disgruntled West Ham crowd. Ledley King scored his first goal in three years, heading in Aaron Lennon's curling cross on 68 minutes before substitute Jamie O'Hara fired in a superb long-range strike in the final minute to wrap up the 2-0 victory.

9th December 2000: In a 3-3 match against Bradford City, Ledley King scored his first goal for Tottenham after just 10 seconds, setting a new Premier League record for the fastest ever goal. It was two seconds quicker than the previous record held jointly by Chris Sutton and the prolific Dwight Yorke. Ledley King's record stood for over 18 years, but has since been broken by Shane Long, who scored for Southampton after just 7.69 seconds in April 2019.

10th December 2015: In a UEFA Europa League group stage match against Monaco, Mauricio Pochettino's team put on a superb display to see them win Group J in style. Cameron Carter-Vickers made his senior debut, having been fast-tracked through the academy. Erik Lamela scored a first-half hat-trick, expertly placing all three of his goals beyond the Monaco keeper, who was having a night to forget. Monaco snatched one back, but Tom Carroll slotted in a neat finish from close-range to round off a perfect 4-1 victory.

11th December 2001: In our biggest ever League Cup win, Spurs beat Bolton Wanderers 6-0 in this thrilling quarter-final. Glenn Hoddle, who saw the Cup as a relatively simple route into Europe, fielded a strong side. Les Ferdinand scored a brilliant 10-minute hat-trick, with the other goals being scored by Simon Davies, Steffen Iversen and an own goal from Bolton. It was sweet revenge for Spurs who had lost 6-2 to Bolton in their only other League Cup meeting five years earlier.

12th December 2005: Tottenham came from a goal behind to beat Portsmouth 3-1 at the Lane. Portsmouth opened the scoring, but Spurs pulled level when Ledley King headed home from a corner. After a Portsmouth handball, Mido converted the awarded penalty in the 85th minute, and substitute Jermain Defoe then wrapped up the 3-1 win.

13th December 2017: Two goals helped Tottenham earn their third home win in a week as they laboured to a 2-0 victory over Brighton at Wembley. Spurs were the better side in the first half but were kept out by stubborn Brighton, until a lucky goal from Serge Aurier in the 40th minute, his first goal for the club. Brighton improved in the second half, but Son Heung-Min secured the win when he headed home with just three minutes to go. Tottenham's uncompromising display was enough to see them move back into the top four.

14th December 2006: Goals from Jermain Defoe and Dimitar Berbatov gave us a comfortable 3-1 victory over Dinamo Bucharest in the UEFA Cup group stages at White Hart Lane. After several near misses, Dimitar Berbatov netted on 16 minutes, smashing in from 20 yards after the Dinamo keeper's poor throw. Jermain Defoe, who had already hit the bar, impressively outpaced the Dinamo defence to add a second before half-time. Just five minutes into the second half, Defoe put us three goals up, but Dinamo managed an injury-time consolation to end the game 3-1. The win secured us top spot in Group B and a place in the knock-out stages of the UEFA Cup. We made it to the quarter-finals where we lost to the ultimate winners Sevilla.

15th December 2018: On a cold and wet December afternoon, a half-full Wembley Stadium endured a goalless 90 minutes in which Spurs made several unsuccessful attempts to break down the Burnley defence. Finally, Christian Eriksen came off the bench to rescue us a 91st-minute winner, so that we could all go home. The win was Mauricio Pochettino 100th Premier League victory as Tottenham manager, our first manager to reach this milestone and the third quickest manager in the Premier League.

16th December 2013: Andre Villas-Boas was dismissed as manager by chairman Daniel Levy after only 18 months in charge. The dismissal followed a string of heavy losses that had started with a 3-0 defeat to West Ham in October and escalated to a 6-0 defeat against Manchester City. A 5-0 thrashing by Liverpool, the club's worst home defeat in 16 years, was the final straw for chairman Daniel Levy, who had spent £107m in the summer transfer window. Despite these results, AVB achieved a percentage win of 59% in Premier League games, more than any other Spurs manager in the Premier League era. A week later, Tottenham announced that Sherwood would take over as the new head coach.

17th December 2015: The planning application for a new £400m, 61,000-seater stadium was finally approved by Haringey Council, more than 7 years after the club first announced plans to build a new stadium. There had been a long delay over the compulsory purchase order of nearby local businesses, with a bitter legal challenge against the order from a local metalworks business. At a planning meeting that began at 7pm and ran through until the early hours, three applications were passed, finally granting planning permission for our new stadium.

18th December 1909: In our first-ever meeting with Chelsea, Billy Minter scored both our goals in a 2-1 win. Tottenham only joined the Football League in 1908 and won promotion to the First Division in 1909. Both Chelsea and Tottenham struggled this season and, in the final match of the season, the two teams met again in a battle to survive relegation. Tottenham won, narrowly avoiding relegation and sending Chelsea down instead.

19th December 2015: Harry Kane made his 100th Spurs appearance in a 2-0 away win at Southampton, who had been struggling in the League. The Saints started well, pressing from the front, but the intensity gave way to sloppiness, as they conceded the match in a three-minute spell before the break. In the 40th minutes, Harry Kane ran through the Saints' defence to coolly slot home, his 10th goal in his last 10 matches. Less than three minutes later, Dele Alli doubled our lead when he took advantage of some lax defending to score from six yards. It was an easy win against a generally struggling Southampton.

20th December 1895: Tottenham Hotspur FC officially became a professional club. To compete with the many other emerging clubs, founding member Robert Buckle proposed that the club should turn professional, a suggestion that was approved following a committee vote.

21st December 1912: Peter McWilliam was appointed manager. The early years of his tenure were disappointing, the club being demoted in 1915 after finishing at the bottom of the First Division. But when football resumed after the War, McWilliam steered the club through one of its most successful periods, being promoted back to the First Division after winning the Second Division title in 1920. He then immediately won the 1921 FA Cup the following year, becoming the first man to win the FA Cup both as a player and a manager. MacWilliam went on to manage Spurs on a second occasion, making him the longest-serving manager at Tottenham, although both his stints were interrupted by war.

22nd December 2013: After the sacking of Andre Villas-Boas earlier that week, a managerless Tottenham beat Southampton 3-2 in an entertaining game. Tim Sherwood was acting temporary manager. Spurs initially fell behind, but Emmanuel Adebayor equalised with a close-range volley. A Southampton own goal after the break gave us the advantage, but Saints levelled back to make it 2-2 before Adebayor curled home the winner. Adebayor had only made one other substitute appearance in the League all season under Villas-Boas, and rewarded Sherwood's faith with two goals. The following day, Sherwood was named as the new head coach.

23rd December 2018: An outstanding performance from Pochettino's side saw us come from behind to beat Everton 6-2 at Goodison Park. In a stunning attacking display, all four of Mauricio Pochettino's forwards were on target, with two goals each for Son Heung-min and Harry Kane, as well as goals from Dele Alli and Christian Eriksen. Everton took the lead, but Spurs quickly made their comeback when Son produced a sublime equaliser from a tight angle. Dele Alli put Spurs ahead, before Harry Kane made it 3-1 when Kieran Trippier's free-kick hit a post and rebounded into Kane's path. A sublime goal from Christian Eriksen extended Tottenham's lead (4-1) before Everton's Gylfi Sigurdsson scored a consolation against his former club (4-2). Son added the fifth, before producing the cross for Kane who left it 6-2. This was only the second time that Tottenham had scored five or more goals against Everton at Goodison Park, the only other time being a 5-2 First Division match in 1928 when Eugene O'Callaghan scored four goals for Spurs.

24th December 1955: A poor start to the season had left Spurs struggling at the bottom of the First Division, and we were desperate for a win. In this home game against Luton Town, Spurs took the lead with two goals from Johnny Brooks and Len Duquemin. Luton pulled one back with 10 minutes to go, but Spurs held on for a 2-1 win. Bobby Smith made his debut in this game, after moving from Chelsea earlier in the month. With 208 goals in 317 appearances, Smith remains Spurs' second-best goal-scorer of all-time, behind Jimmy Greaves.

25th December 1956: Back in the 1950s, teams would play two League games between Christmas Eve and Boxing Day, and so games on Christmas day were very normal. On this particular Christmas, Spurs fans celebrated a very merry Christmas when they beat Everton 6-0 at White Hart Lane, with goals from Tommy Harmer (penalty), Terry Medwin (2), Bobby Smith (2) and Alfie Stokes.

26th December 2012: Bale scored his first Spurs hat-trick in a 4-0 away win against Aston Villa. Tottenham was superior in every department and could have inflicted much more damage in the first half were it not for Villa's superb goalkeeping. After the break, Jermain Defoe finally got the goal Spurs deserved. From that moment on, the floodgates opened and Spurs continued to score with embarrassing ease, with Bale seizing his first hat-trick for the club.

27th December 2011: Another two goals from Gareth Bale gave Spurs a comfortable 2-0 away win at Norwich. The first goal came in the 55th minute. Scott Parker, Rafael Van der Vaart and Emmanuel Adebayor had done all the hard work, leaving Bale to chip home from 10 yards out. Then 12 minutes later, a trademark break from Tottenham, instigated by Modric, allowed Bale to make a searing run down the pitch that took him clear of the Norwich defence, before scoring right over the head of the Norwich keeper.

28th December 1998: Bow down to Armstrong. An opening goal from Les Ferdinand, followed by a second-half hat-trick from Chris Armstrong, saw Spurs beat Everton 4-1. By 62 minutes, the game that appeared to be heading for a 1-1 stalemate, until Armstrong shot Tottenham into a 2-1 lead. Having got his eye in, Armstrong was clearly on a roll, scoring another two in an exceptional 20 minute period. Two minutes from the end of Tottenham's best victory of the season, Chris Armstrong was substituted off. On his way to the touchline, Armstrong was stopped by David Ginola, who, in a memorable scene, bowed down to his formidable teammate.

29th December 2007: In an entertaining game against Reading at White Hart Lane, Spurs came back from a goal down three times to ultimately win the game 6-4. Dimitar Berbatov scored four of our goals, recording his first Premier League hat-trick. Tottenham looked the more confident from the start, and after just seven minutes, Berbatov volleyed in his first from a Robbie Keane pass. Reading equalised after a howler from Paul Robinson, but the real drama came after the break. Reading took the lead in the 53rd minute and Spurs manager Juande Ramos reacted by replacing Ledley King with Jermain Defoe. It was an excellent decision and from that moment on there was barely a second that passed by without incident, as seven more goals were scored in 20 minutes. Berbatov smashed home his second for an equaliser, and Reading restored their lead, but Berbatov was back again to complete his hat-trick. Yet again, Reading went ahead, before Steed Malbranque equalised to make it 4-4. Keane was awarded a penalty, and although his spot-kick was saved, Defoe headed in the rebound to put Spurs into the lead. Berbatov then struck in another powerful strike seven minutes from time to leave the score at 6-4.

30th December 1972: A 4-3 aggregate win in the League Cup semi-finals against Wolves earnt Spurs a place in their second League Cup Final. Martin Peters scored in both games. Spurs held a one-goal lead from the first leg, but with Terry Naylor conceding an own goal in the first minute of this second leg, Spurs had to fight all the way. Martin Peters got one for Spurs, but Wolves came back in the final minute. The nerve-wracking match went into extra time, with Spurs keeping the pressure on the Wolves, whose keeper made several outstanding saves. Finally, in the 113th minute, Martin Chivers hammered in the winner, to take Spurs into the final.

31st December 2011: In the last game of the year, Rafael van der Vaart put Spurs ahead when he hit in Benoit Assou-Ekotto's cross just before the interval. After the break, Swansea piled on the pressure and they equalised when Brad Friedel fumbled a deflected cross six minutes from time. Having lost only one League game since the end of August, Spurs headed into the New Year as London's top club for the first time since 1995.

Printed in Great Britain
by Amazon

29657101R00064